Rhonda Watson has done us all a favou[r] death she bravely shares with us her h[ome] important questions of life and Christia[n] disabled person I found this book authe[ntic,] helpful, encouraging and challenging. I warmly recommend it to anyone who is suffering.
Dr Emily Ackerman, author of A Time to Care: Loving Your Elderly Parents

The complex and difficult interface between serious illness and serious faith is explored here with no holds barred. It is searingly honest but also positive in the most God-honouring, Bible-driven, emotionally authentic way. A truly helpful read for anyone struggling under a king-sized burden – or supporting someone else. In fact I think almost all Christians would do well to read it. I found *Remember* deeply moving and empowering, and will be recommending it to many folk.
Julian Hardyman, Senior Pastor, Eden Baptist Church, Cambridge

This is a book about dealing with suffering. Therefore it is a book for everyone. Searingly honest and quietly confident, Watson invites us to take the stories of our lives and submit them to the grander story of the gospel of Jesus Christ. Watson speaks with passion and elegance and joy. She longs for us to sink more deeply into God's word and his grace-filled relationship with us. This book does just that.
Graham Stanton, Principal, Youthworks training college, Sydney

INTER-VARSITY PRESS
Norton Street, Nottingham NG7 3HR, England
Email: ivp@ivpbooks.com
Website: www.ivpbooks.com

First published 2011

British Library Cataloguing in Publication Data
A catalogue record for this book is available from the British Library.

ISBN: 978–1–84474–545–6

Set in Myriad 12/17pt
Typeset in Great Britain by CRB Associates, Potterhanworth, Lincolnshire
Printed and bound in Great Britain by Ashford Colour Press Ltd, Gosport, Hampshire

Inter-Varsity Press publishes Christian books that are true to the Bible and that communicate the gospel, develop discipleship and strengthen the church for its mission in the world.

Inter-Varsity Press is closely linked with the Universities and Colleges Christian Fellowship, a student movement connecting Christian Unions in universities and colleges throughout Great Britain, and a member movement of the International Fellowship of Evangelical Students. Website: www.uccf.org.uk

Rhonda Watson

Remember

... the things that matter
when hope is hard to find

ivp

For Gary, best friend and carer

Acknowledgments

Family and friends have supported me in prayer, persistent cheerfulness, notes of encouragement, and with hefty containers of pumpkin soup. Thank you.

Contents

Foreword

In times of trial and suffering, especially when the end of the tunnel seems distant, we may react in one of two ways: either we can sink into despair and frustration, looking down to the 'cellar' of our life, or we can lift up our eyes to the 'attic', where we contemplate a wider horizon, a new vision of our personal tragedies. *Remember* is an amazing example of the second attitude.

Rhonda Watson writes with the sensitivity of a tender heart, tested in the furnace of trial, and the wisdom of someone who has learned to depend utterly on God for her daily portion of strength. I greatly appreciate the combination of the subjective – her own feelings and experience – with the objective truths of the Scriptures. The book is constantly rooted in the Word, thus avoiding a merely subjective approach to suffering which is so popular today as a result of Eastern religious influence.

Remember provides not only godly inspiration, but also a practical way to talk to yourself and master your thoughts and emotions in times of distress. The presentation in each chapter of a pair of opposite realities – beauty and ugliness, silence and speech, and so on – reminds us of the spiritual battle inside, and the need to lift up the eyes of faith so that, like Moses, we may 'endure as seeing Him who is invisible' (Hebrews 11:27). Beautifully written, each chapter ends with a prayer, a summary and a space for your personal reflection, which greatly help the reader to apply new insights to their own life.

As the author of a book on suffering and finding myself often under the fire of trial, I cannot think of a better devotional reading for anyone coping with painful situations. I warmly commend *Remember*, with the conviction that the reader will feel renewed and encouraged by every single page.

Dr Pablo Martinez, psychiatrist, and author of *A Thorn in the Flesh: Finding Strength and Hope Amid Suffering*

Preface

This book is an account of my experience of dealing with Motor Neurone Disease. I share a little of the physical aspects of adapting to this disease, but mostly I share my inner journey. Doctors and therapists routinely ask me about my physical symptoms and needs. I have found that hardly anyone asks me about the emotional and spiritual challenges I face. In many ways this is the most acute need I feel. How am I to make sense of my experience? How am I to make peace with the sense of loss? How am I to be real in my relationship with God? These were the questions that drove me as I wrote this book. At first it was written to myself and I had no thought of others reading it. As I reached the end of 'talking to myself', it occurred to me that others might benefit. If you are reading this, then I am thankful that God has used this book for others, and I pray for your encouragement, in whatever circumstances you find yourself.

Rhonda Watson, November 2010

'Has God forgotten to be merciful?
   Has he in anger withheld his compassion?'

Then I thought, 'To this I will appeal:
   the years of the right hand of the Most High.'
I will remember the deeds of the Lord;
   yes, I will remember your miracles of long ago.
I will meditate on all your works
   and consider all your mighty deeds.

(Psalm 77:9–12, my emphasis)

So I will always remind you of these things, even though you know them and are firmly established in the truth you now have. I think it is right to refresh your memory as long as I live in the tent of this body, because I know that I will soon put it aside, as our Lord Jesus Christ has made clear to me. And I will make every effort to see that after my departure you will always be able to **remember these things**.

(2 Peter 1:12–15, my emphasis)

Introduction

'Has God forgotten to be merciful?
Has he in anger withheld
his compassion?'
(Psalm 77:9)

There are times when these words from Psalm 77 echo our own deepest questions, whether we verbalize them or not. When we are struggling with uncertainty and hurt we may cry out to God: Have you forgotten me? Where is your compassion? Are you there at all?

Everyone has their own story. Everyone has their own struggles. It's never helpful to compare, to wonder whose story is the worst, who carries the most sorrow and who has dealt with the deepest disappointments. Your struggle is real and heavy right now; mine is real and heavy right now. You bring your story and your pain to this moment. I will share with you some of my story and my questions, and my struggle may resonate with yours. Together, let's remember. Let us try to remember what really matters when life is a struggle, when hope slips away and when our hearts tremble with sorrow and weariness.

After eighteen months of small strange symptoms, in October 2008 I was diagnosed with Motor Neurone Disease (MND). In my case it was labelled 'bulbar onset' which means that the mouth, throat and face area was where the disease was most obvious. It affected my speech, chewing and swallowing, and facial muscles. It grew to include neck and shoulders, feet, and legs. My most noticeable symptoms in the first year involved speaking; in short, I lost my voice.

At the time of diagnosis, I was in a busy leadership role as part of Youthworks in Sydney, and I also did some lecturing at the Youthworks training college. I was preparing to work with teachers in Christian schools, providing professional development to teachers, and helping to bring a Christian perspective into all areas of school life. Everything I did and hoped to do involved speaking.

From a personal perspective I experienced many consequences. Firstly, I was unable to work. This might sound good to some fifty-five-year-olds, but I loved my work. It filled me with energy and I thrived on the relationships, busyness, challenges, and usefulness. It was a great loss to me to be unable to do all this.

In a family context, my most poignant moment, which forced me to face the reality of what was happening, was simply being unable to read a picture book with my four-year-old grandson. I could no longer phone my ageing parents to check on how they were. I couldn't chat with my children, make jokes, and laugh with friends. I began to avoid social situations, especially one-on-one, as I couldn't converse.

Some months passed and all these experiences became set in concrete. For the first months I fought it, denied it, and decided I would carry on anyway. I even kept trying to speak – to the embarrassment of the listeners. Then, on my fifty-sixth birthday I decided it was time to acquiesce. From that day I would no longer speak. I would let go of my previous life and accept that I really was sick and my life would never be the same again. I would stop the ways in which I was trying to distract myself, face the grief of it all and give in to reality.

Of course this involved a deep sense of sadness and loss, but I just sat with that for some time. It was an essential step in facing the reality of my new life. But I was also longing to know if there was anything useful I could be doing. I feared that if I had no project, no purpose, I would sink into depression and despair.

One night as I read about the letters of Seneca, the Roman Stoic philosopher, to fictitious recipients, I thought I needed to write myself some 'letters'. I needed to remind myself what I believed, why it mattered and in the process work out how I was supposed to live in this disabled and chronically ill state. What was my current 'occupation'? What territory did I 'occupy' now and how could I live faithfully in a way that honoured Jesus in this new and strange territory? So, I began to write the following chapters to remind myself about what gave my life meaning. Strangely, I needed to 'speak' to myself. It's hard to explain but words keep happening in my mind and yet none are spoken. At times it's raucous and loud in there, and feels like a pent-up river. So I hoped that putting some words out there on the page would ease the sense of overload.

These comments by Dr Martyn Lloyd-Jones proved helpful. He explains the importance of talking to ourselves.

I say that we must talk to ourselves, instead of allowing 'ourselves' to talk to us! Do you realize what that means? I suggest that the main trouble in this whole matter of spiritual depression in a sense is this, that we allow our self to talk to us instead of talking to ourself. Am I just trying to be deliberately paradoxical? Have you realized that most of your unhappiness in life is due to the fact that you are listening to yourself instead of talking to yourself?

Take those thoughts that come to you the moment you wake up in the morning. You have not originated them, but they start talking to you, they bring back the problems of yesterday. Somebody is talking. Who is talking to you? Your self is talking to you.

Now [the psalmist's] treatment was this; instead of allowing this self to talk to him, he starts talking to himself. 'Why art thou cast down o my soul?' he asks.

And then you must go on to remind yourself of God, who he is, and what God is, and what God has done, and what God has pledged himself to do. Then having done that, end on this great note: defy yourself, and defy other people, and defy the devil and the whole world, and say with this man: 'I shall yet praise him for the help of his countenance.'[1]

(Dr Martyn Lloyd-Jones)

This little book is my response and my effort to 'talk to myself' wisely, gently and yet very firmly; and it is what I need to hear, some days I *desperately* need to hear these truths.

At the heart of my experience of this sickness, and the inevitability of decline and death, is a face-to-face relationship with God and the bewilderment, struggle and questioning I feel towards him. I write about joy, trust, thankfulness but, oh, how I struggle to be joyful, trusting and thankful. This is no shout-out-loud victory I feel, rather a deep, 'and yet' determination towards joy, trust and thankfulness. In fact each chapter was quite a struggle to write because I had to keep looking God in the face, determined to ask my questions, cry my tears and work it out.

Professor Richard Mouw tells of some Dutch villagers faced with tragedy who taught their baffled pastor to face God in this way. The pastor struggled to make connections with them as they mourned their loss. Gently, they rebuked him saying, '"Minister, no stranger did that to us." 'The face they looked upon was God's face. It was no stranger who had done this to them. It was the God whom they worshipped and trusted. Their faith in a loving God was being tested, but it was not being undermined.'[2] Therefore they continued to pray, to trust, and to worship.

A close friend often reminds me, 'we have an audience of One'. It is, as the Dutch theologian Abraham Kuyper said, *coram deo*, 'being before the face of God'.[3] Being silent, isolated, and fatigued has forced me to live mostly away from the company of others. So my days, and my unspoken words, are 'before the face of God' more than they have ever been before.

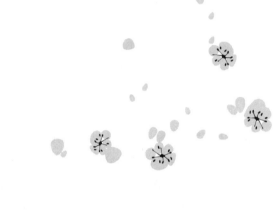

Beauty and ugliness

On the cross, in Jesus himself,
we see the meeting place
of perfect beauty
and absolute ugliness.

Most middle-aged people in the developed world worry about their deteriorating appearance. We have so much to eat that we become flabby; we have so much leisure time that we tend to sit and watch TV for hours each day; we have enough money to spend it on self-indulgent distractions. All of this is a completely counterproductive cycle. The flabbier we become the more time we spend watching TV which is filled with young, slim, beautiful (and botoxed) young people. We are taunted into spending more money on products to 'stop' ageing, or clothes to disguise our flab, or low-calorie food to get rid of our flab.

Each morning we look in our mirrors and assess the wrinkles, the sags, and the ill-fitting clothes. Our spirits sink and we carry away a sense of inadequacy and sadness, probably trying to comfort ourselves with some chocolate.

In the case of a disability, or chronic illness, these experiences are increased. That's how it feels to me. My face won't smile properly anymore. I have lost any ability to be sparkling and witty, and I spend most days alone so who is there to impress with new clothes and make-up?

So I have been wondering: What is ugliness? What is beauty? Does being 'beautiful' really matter?

I recall Gerard Manley Hopkins' poem, 'Pied Beauty':

Pied Beauty
Glory be to God for dappled things –
For skies of couple-colour as a brinded cow;
For rose-moles in all stipple upon trout that swim;
Fresh-firecoal chestnut-falls; finches' wings;
Landscape plotted and pieced – fold, fallow, and plough;
And all trades, their gear and tackle and trim.
All things counter, original, spare, strange;
Whatever is fickle, freckled (who knows how?)
With swift, slow; sweet, sour; adazzle, dim;

He fathers-forth whose beauty is past change:
Praise him.[1]

(Gerard Manley Hopkins, 1884–1889)

Hopkins sees the things that are dappled, different, unusual, 'strange' as things which bring glory to God. Their very strangeness is cause for praise to their Creator. He sees something that strikes him as beautiful and praises its maker. He who 'fathers-forth' is the only one whose beauty is 'past change'. The speckled, imperfect, unusual, and dappled creatures are as they are; it is in the Creator that beauty is found. He is Beauty.

How helpful this is as I consider the issue of beauty and ugliness. We so easily become self-absorbed. We look at the mirror, the wardrobe, and the scales. We wonder endlessly about how others see us. We look and peer at one another: Is she getting fatter? Is he ageing well? Are her jeans too tight? Is she successful? Is he still going to the gym? Does he need glasses?

In our very human foolishness we remain self-centred. Hopkins says to us: look at him who is Beauty itself, praise him for all his works, and seek wisdom about beauty and ugliness in relation to Him.

It makes me think about the way many Christians these days present the gospel, even Jesus himself, as being there for our benefit. One step into your local Christian bookshop and it slams you in the face. It seems that God exists so that I can feel better about myself, can be happy, blessed, fulfilled, beautiful, prosperous, captivating, in control of my spending, slim, a successful parent, and so on, and so on.

I need to turn to God's Word to sort this out, because truth be told, I *want* to read the books, I *want* to be captivating, I *want* to be slim and rich, I *want* to be healed. Of course I do, because I'm basically as silly as everyone else if I'm not careful.

The psalmist, David, longs to see true beauty, and he doesn't seek it in his mirror.

One thing I ask of the LORD,
    this is what I seek:
that I may dwell in the house of the LORD
    all the days of my life,
to gaze upon the beauty of the LORD
    and to seek him in his temple.

(Psalm 27:4)

This psalm focuses on the Lord – his beauty, faithfulness, mercy, goodness. It reminds me to respond by gazing upon his beauty, seeking his face, and trusting him. This sweeps away my self-absorption with a gust of fresh air. My gaze is where it should be – on his beauty; my security is where it should be – in his faithfulness and power; my longings are where they should be – for him.

There is another side to God's beauty. It is not pink and floral, not cloying and sentimental, not weak and pathetic.

The Mighty One, God, the Lord,
    speaks and summons the earth
    from the rising of the sun to the place where it sets.
From Zion, perfect in beauty,
    God shines forth.
Our God comes and will not be silent;
    a fire devours before him,
    and around him a tempest rages.

(Psalm 50:1–3)

This is 'don't mess with me' beauty. This is not to be under-estimated or taken for granted beauty. It's thunderous, fearful, radiant, and strong. This is holy beauty cloaked in sovereign power. This is beauty that speaks! This beauty would be un-approachable, except for one thing. Except for Jesus.

It is in Jesus that we may truly see Beauty. And yet there is a para-dox here. He is beautiful in so many ways: perfectly sinless, deeply compassionate, lovingly self-sacrificing, wise, true, life-giving. But he is also harsh with hypocrites, he tells stories that confuse, and he makes outlandish claims about himself, embarrassingly ridiculous claims it might seem, 'lock him up in rehab' kinds of claims.

None of his beauty is about his appearance. Isaiah prophesied that those who saw him would hardly notice what he looked like. This is strange to me. The Son of God, full of power and wisdom, sinless and compassionate, is ordinary-looking. He would actually be embarrassing to look at, someone you would instinctively turn away from.

He grew up before him like a tender shoot,
    and like a root out of dry ground.
He had no beauty or majesty to attract us to him,
    nothing in his appearance that we should desire him.
He was despised and rejected by men,
    a man of sorrows, and familiar with suffering.
Like one from whom men hide their faces
    he was despised, and we esteemed him not.

Surely he took up our infirmities
   and carried our sorrows,
yet we considered him stricken by God,
   smitten by him, and afflicted.

(Isaiah 53:2–4)

Isaiah said that worse than ordinary-looking, people would want to hide their faces so they could not see him. He would be so humiliated, so despised, and such an object of horror that people would try to avoid seeing him at all.

All this happened on the cross. Here the man of such deep and strong beauty became a man despicable and awful to see. Here is the meeting place of perfect beauty and absolute ugliness. It's a paradox. He sacrificed his life-giving beauty and accepted deathly ugliness. And yet at that very moment he was most beautiful, most glorious. He said to his disciples: 'Now is the Son of Man glorified and God is glorified in him.'[2]

The resurrection morning proclaimed the victory of beauty, truth, life, and righteousness over ugliness, death, and sin. In John's narrative there is a moment when the victory is expressed in the context of a relationship and at a moment of deep grief. Are there any more beautiful words than those between Mary and Jesus by the empty tomb?

Then the disciples went back to their homes, but Mary stood outside the tomb crying. As she wept, she bent over to look into the tomb and saw two angels in white, seated where Jesus' body had been, one at the head and the other at the foot.

They asked her, 'Woman, why are you crying?'

'They have taken my Lord away,' she said, 'and I don't know where they have put him.' At this, she turned around and saw Jesus standing there, but she did not realise that it was Jesus.

'Woman,' he said, 'why are you crying? Who is it you are looking for?'

Thinking he was the gardener, she said, 'Sir, if you have

carried him away, tell me where you have put him, and I will get him.'

Jesus said to her, 'Mary.'

She turned toward him and cried out in Aramaic, 'Rabboni!' (which means Teacher).

(John 20:10–16)

The resurrection of Jesus is a beautiful moment of sweet victory over all that is marred and wrecked by sin. It means that death itself has been defeated. For those who are in Christ, his victory becomes our victory. His resurrection means I will be resurrected. His death was sufficient to deal with my sin. My ugliness will be removed by his beauty.

So it will be with the resurrection of the dead. The body that is sown is perishable, it is raised imperishable; it is sown in dishonour, it is raised in glory; it is sown in weakness, it is raised in power; it is sown a natural body, it is raised a spiritual body.

(1 Corinthians 15:42–44)

Now what was that I was worried about when I glimpsed myself in the mirror? Nothing worth mentioning.

Jesus came for people just like me and you: broken, marred, imperfect, decaying, and diseased; those with broken bodies and wounded spirits; captives, living dark and difficult lives. Isaiah promised a day would come for people like us, because a person would come for people like us.

> The Spirit of the Sovereign Lord is on me,
>   because the Lord has anointed me
>   to preach good news to the poor.
> He has sent me to bind up the broken-hearted,
>   to proclaim freedom for the captives
>   and release from darkness for the prisoners,
> to proclaim the year of the Lord's favour
>   and the day of vengeance of our God,
> to comfort all who mourn,
>   and provide for those who grieve in Zion –

to bestow on them a crown of beauty
    instead of ashes,
the oil of gladness
    instead of mourning,
and a garment of praise
    instead of a spirit of despair.
They will be called oaks of righteousness,
    a planting of the LORD
    for the display of his splendour.

(Isaiah 61:1–3)

Jesus read these words in the synagogue at Nazareth and declared: 'Today this scripture is fulfilled in your hearing.'[3] In him I will receive a crown of beauty to replace my ashes of sickness and death; in him I will be seen as an oak of righteousness, for the display of his splendour, his beauty. What a day when this is completed, when the groaning birth pangs of the present age result in new life and the full redemption of our bodies.[4] Beautiful day!

It is that beautiful day I am being prepared for now. More than simply waiting, I am actively getting ready. God is at work to complete what he has begun in me.

> . . . being confident of this, that he who began a good work in you will carry it on to completion until the day of Christ Jesus.
>
> (Philippians 1:6)

The getting ready involves things that feel ugly, painful, and wrong. They are just the journey to complete beauty.

> When, through fiery trials thy pathway shall lie,
> His grace, all-sufficient, shall be thy supply;
> The flames shall not hurt thee, His only design
> They dross to consume and thy gold to refine.[5]
>
> (Richard Keen, c. 1787)

Prayer

Lord of beauty and grace, teach me to gaze at you.

When I am bereft because of the ugliness within me and the brokenness around me,

Give me hope, peace, courage, and good humour.

Let me wait well for your return.

Let me trust you in the times of shadow and fear,

Let me have your joy in the times of grief and the temptation to despair.

Let me be truly beautiful, for the sake of your glory.

Remember …

It is good to lift our eyes from the ugliness of our situation and to gaze with awe on the beauty of the Lord.

Reject the world's preoccupation with outward signs of beauty.

Turn to God's Word to gain God's perspective about beauty and ugliness.

Let go of self-absorption and be captivated by Jesus – his beauty, faithfulness, and power.

Remember the gospel message which tells us that our sinful ugliness is replaced by Jesus' beautiful righteousness.

Reflect

two

Silence and speech

I look forward to the day when,
with healed tongue,
I will sing and praise my Saviour.
On that day my silence will be over.

I have been thinking about silence. Those who are sick, disabled, poor, and needy often feel silenced by those around them. It seems that the powerful, successful, rich, and strong have all the speaking time they need and plenty of people ready to listen. Others of us are forced into passive, quiet places, becoming onlookers, robbed of our voices.

I mumbled to my husband yesterday, 'I have become your silent companion.' I tend to avoid faces, keep my eyes averted, and look away to avoid the embarrassment of having to try to answer someone. Meeting old Meg at the local shop last week, I couldn't make her understand my words as I 'said', 'I can't speak to you, I'm sorry. I can't speak.' She couldn't read my piece of paper that said 'I can't speak but I can hear and understand.' She was annoyed and confused as she tried to make contact; I was increasingly embarrassed and frustrated. My alternative is to never leave the house. Not a good option, but there are days when it's tempting.

I am silent now. It is a very strange experience to have so many words and thoughts bubbling and interacting in my mind, and yet not be able to say anything. No one knows whether I am alert, intelligent, and thoughtful. No one can hear me anymore, except God.

People from the past come to mind. I remember Julia, the typesetter I worked with years ago. She was profoundly deaf, and she would try to speak and I would try to understand and to speak back. How self-congratulatory I was, thinking, poor Julia I bet she's glad to have me as a friend because I try to speak to her, I finish sentences for her. I used to write on paper what others were saying so she might be able to follow conversations around her. I was condescending and patronizing. Now I know how she felt. Sorry, Julia. How I hate it when people do that for me now.

Of course, Millie the dog understands me. She is the only one I speak with freely. I can make a mumble of sounds to her and she responds with a look of trust and comprehension, and I pretend she knows what I said. I think of Wilson, the volleyball that Tom Hanks' character, Chuck, dressed up in the film *Cast Away*. Wilson was crucial to Chuck's mental health, and those of us who saw the film all understood his deep need to speak to someone who would listen. More recently, there was the character of Fred in the film *I am Legend* starring Will Smith as Robert Neville, apparently the sole survivor of a mysterious pandemic. Fred was the shop dummy that Robert spoke to each day because he had seen no other humans for three years. I remember the day after his dog died, when he went up to a female shop dummy, and pleaded with her, so softly and sadly, 'Please answer me, please. Please speak to me.' The need to speak, to be listened to, and to be answered, is deeply human.

I think of Beethoven and his genius, creating music in his mind and writing it down so it could be played and heard over and over again. His music is so beautiful, strong, passionate, intricate, and souring. Imagine his despair as his deafness grew. He still had so much music to create; but little time to hear it. He kept creating, but didn't hear it. He heard music in his mind but silence all around him; I hear words in my mind but only scribble them in silence to others. I think of others who may feel 'voiceless' in different ways, for example, those who stutter, or feel unconfident, or marginalized. You may have your own experience of losing a key part of who you are to illness or disability.

Just now I hear doves' wings as they descend to the ground, a whip bird off in the tree tops, magpie morning song, squawking cockatoos, trills from rosellas, arguing lorikeets. It's all just outside my window. Within the house there's a heater buzzing softly, a washing machine spinning and draining, a dog scampering, and my tapping on the computer keyboard. I don't really endure silence, but I can't break it with my voice. I can't sing, say poetry, play my recorder, phone someone, laugh, or cry softly. All my sound-making is marred and faulty. I can't afford to dwell on it too much or despair will come and taunt me, but I can't say 'I love you' clearly anymore; I can't read a story to my grandson; I can't joke with my children; I can't chuckle at a film or teach or lead a service or pray out loud. That's my form of enforced silence.

Although I pray for a sense of quiet contentment and trust through all this, there's also a sense of fury at times. There's anger at this disability. I love the first verse of Alfred Tennyson's poem 'Break, Break, Break':

> Break, break, break
> On thy cold grey stones, O sea!
> And I would that my tongue could utter
> The thoughts that arise in me![1]

(Alfred Tennyson, 1809–1892)

His words express my longing for a tongue to utter the thoughts that arise in me. And it's right that I should rage against this condition, as it's another aspect of the groaning creation, waiting for the day of healing and redemption and the final victory of Jesus in making all things new. Meanwhile, I am forced to confront the discomforting fact that this comes to me from God's sovereign hand.

Moses had a speech problem, well so he thought anyway. He wanted to turn down the offer of being God's spokesman to Pharaoh:

> The LORD said to him, 'Who gave man his mouth? Who makes him deaf or mute? Who gives him sight or makes him blind? Is it not I, the LORD? Now go; I will help you speak and will teach you what to say.'
> But Moses said, 'O Lord, please send someone else to do it.'
> (Exodus 4:11–13)

As part of the mystery of suffering I have to confront the fact that God allowed this disease in my life. I must even learn to say that he decreed it; he sent it; he purposed it before I was born.

That is uncomfortable, but I'd better deal with it, because the alternative is unthinkable and unbiblical.

God is not cruel and vindictive, but he is sovereign. He is not heartless and careless in the way he deals with us, he is full of compassion. We simply don't see the full picture. Job is a good example to us. Suffering came into his life – but not without God's overruling in the matter. Satan never had a free reign, God maintained his sovereignty. Job knew none of what was going on behind the scenes, he only felt his pain and grief.

What has he sent into your life? How uncomfortable it is to see our struggles this way, delivered to us from God's hand. It's confronting and makes it hard to look God in the face honestly. It's part of the deep mystery of suffering we all struggle to understand, both logically and emotionally.

On the other hand, we know God means to deal with this, and all the brokenness of his world and his people. The following wonderful words from Isaiah now have a personal impact. They were written to exiles to give them hope for the future, a future where God would act to bring in his kingdom and redeem them. This is the vision of the fullness of the kingdom of God, the Day of the Lord:

> The desert and the parched land will be glad;
>> the wilderness will rejoice and blossom.
> Like the crocus, it will burst into bloom;
>> it will rejoice greatly and shout for joy.
> The glory of Lebanon will be given to it,
>> the splendour of Carmel and Sharon;
> they will see the glory of the LORD,
>> the splendour of our God.

> Strengthen the feeble hands,
>> steady the knees that give way;
> say to those with fearful hearts,
>> 'Be strong, do not fear;

your God will come,
    he will come with vengeance;
with divine retribution
    he will come to save you.'

Then will the eyes of the blind be opened
    and the ears of the deaf unstopped.
Then will the lame leap like a deer,
    and the mute tongue shout for joy.
Water will gush forth in the wilderness
    and streams in the desert . . .

No lion will be there,
    nor will any ferocious beast get up on it;
    they will not be found there.
But only the redeemed will walk there,
    and the ransomed of the Lord will return.
They will enter Zion with singing;
    everlasting joy will crown their heads.

Gladness and joy will overtake them,
    and sorrow and sighing will flee away.

(Isaiah 35:1–6, 9–10)

I know this will happen. I know that my muteness will be healed. For the first time these words from Isaiah are close to home, so close to home. I know they will be fulfilled because the day of the kingdom has already dawned. The kingdom has dawned in Jesus.

Listen to the peal of victory in Jesus' words:

'There will be no more death or mourning or crying or pain, for the old order of things has passed away.' He who was seated on the throne said: 'I am making everything new!'

(Revelation 21:4–5)

> Great crowds came to him, bringing the lame, the blind, the crippled, the mute, and many others, and laid them at his feet; and he healed them. The people were amazed when they saw the mute speaking, the crippled made well, the lame walking, and the blind seeing. And they praised the God of Israel.
>
> (Matthew 15:30–31)

These signs reassure me that the kingdom has dawned, the King has arrived, and the hope of renewal is sure. His resurrection sealed my hope. His ascension is like the overture of the symphony to come. So I can wait with hope and courage, even if I am silent in my waiting. There will be a day when 'the mute will shout for joy' and I look forward to that day with excitement.

Meanwhile I live with silence. There are many important things that are silent, or so quiet one can hardly hear them. 'As quietly as trees in spring' says the Austrian poet, Rainer Maria Rilke, in his wonderful poem, 'The quieting of Mary with the resurrected one'. Hardly a word is spoken in this dramatic moment between Mary and her Risen Lord. 'Mary' says Jesus, and that word is enough; it contains all the wonder of resurrection, all the hope needed to dispel despair, all the truth of victory.[2]

The quieting of Mary with the resurrected one

What they felt then: is it not
above all other mysteries the sweetest
and yet still earthly:
when he, pale from the grave,
his burdens laid down, went to her:
risen in all places.
Oh, first to her. How they
inexpressibly began to heal.
Yes, to heal: that simple. They felt no need
to touch each other strongly.
He placed his hand, which next
would be eternal, for scarcely
a second on her womanly shoulder.

And they began
quietly as trees in spring
in infinite simultaneity
their season
of ultimate communing. [3]

(Rainer Maria Rilke, 1875–1926)

What else happens 'quietly as trees in spring'? A loving look between old friends, the first sip of morning coffee, a baby's smile, a flower opening, autumn leaves, Thai chilli chicken hitting the taste buds, a king parrot swooping, a whale surfacing, the tides, a full moon, prayer, death, breathing, drowning, a baby's first moment, a child's first steps, and old men remembering.

In the end, what matters is that *God* speaks, he is not silent. He spoke promises to Abraham. He spoke to Moses from a burning bush and on a mountaintop. He spoke to his prophets. Finally, conclusively, he spoke in the very person of his Son, Jesus.[4]

God spoke creation into being: 'And God said . . . And it was so.'[5] God spoke through his prophets. God took the initiative with his people: choosing them, blessing them, redeeming them, giving them law and promise. He spoke to warn and punish, to reassure and strengthen. His words dominate the story of salvation. The words of his people, in comparison, were fickle, shallow, and unreliable. God pleaded with them, 'Fix these words of mine in your hearts and minds . . . ':[6]

> Be careful, or you will be enticed to turn away and
> worship other gods and bow down to them . . . Fix
> these words of mine in your hearts and minds; tie them
> as symbols on your hands and bind them on your
> foreheads. Teach them to your children, talking about
> them when you sit at home and when you walk along
> the road, when you lie down and when you get up. Write
> them on the door-frames of your houses and on your gates,
> so that your days and the days of your children may be

many in the land that the Lord swore to give your
forefathers, as many as the days that the heavens are above
the earth.

(Deuteronomy 11:16–21)

They didn't fix his words in their hearts and minds. In the
face of human rebellion and hardness of heart, God acted in
grace to save. He himself came to be among them. To speak first
hand, through the mouth of a man, a breathing, swallowing,
speaking man. The God-Man, the man of glory and grace and
truth: Jesus.

In the beginning was the Word, and the Word was with
God, and the Word was God. He was with God in the
beginning.

Through him all things were made; without him nothing
was made that has been made. In him was life, and that life
was the light of men. The light shines in the darkness, but the
darkness has not understood it.

> The Word became flesh and made his dwelling among us.
> We have seen his glory, the glory of the One and Only, who
> came from the Father, full of grace and truth.
>
> (John 1:1–5, 14)

His disciples, like us, bewildered and weak, also knew him as the one who had the words they needed. 'You have the words of eternal life'[7] proclaims Peter.

So, in the end, my silence and wordlessness is not that important. God speaks; he speaks through his Son. He speaks to me. It is enough to listen. I look forward to the day when, with healed tongue, I will sing and praise my Saviour. On that day my silence will be over.

You may have a different longing that will be satisfied on that day. Your struggle will be different, your grief personal, and your disappointments embedded in your own story. Still, join with me in listening to our speaking God and be full of hope at the joy and healing that is to come. Let this ease your trials now, and we'll wait together.

Come, let us join our cheerful songs

Come, let us join our cheerful songs
With angels round the throne;
Ten thousand thousand are their tongues,
But all their joys are one.

'Worthy the Lamb that died,' they cry,
'To be exalted thus.'
'Worthy the Lamb,' our lips reply,
'For He was slain for us.'

Jesus is worthy to receive
Honour and power divine:
And blessings, more than we can give,
Be, Lord, for ever Thine.

Let all that dwell above the sky,
And air, and earth, and seas,
Conspire to lift Thy glories high,
And speak Thine endless praise.

The whole creation join in one
To bless the sacred name
Of him that sits upon the throne
And to adore the Lamb.[8]

(Isaac Watts, 1674–1748)

Prayer

O Holy Spirit, voice of the mute,
Send my praise to his throne;
Give words to my thankfulness;
Assert my trust;
Answer his 'Mine!' with 'Yours!'
Speak for me when my words fail.

Remember …

*God speaks to us. Jesus is God's perfect word to us. One day we
will lift our voices in perfect praise.*

Face the truth that God has allowed this suffering into my life.

Hold fast to the truth that God is sovereign and compassionate –
even if we can't make sense of it all.

Take heart because the new kingdom has dawned in Jesus.

Have hope because Jesus' resurrection confirms the coming of the day
when all brokenness will be healed.

Reflect

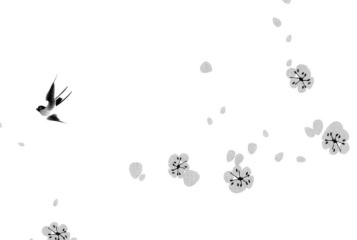

three

Fear and trust

We have a daily choice:
Do we stoke our fear,
or settle it?

To be human is to feel fear. It is as much a part of life as hunger and thirst. For some of us, fear has become layered year after year, hurt after hurt. Most of us prefer busy distraction to facing fear and admitting it. But often, things happen in our lives that force us to stop and be honest and face our fears.

When I was first diagnosed with MND, I felt a terrible fear. I struggled with this fear, but I was not able at first to understand exactly what I was afraid of. For some months I was driven to 'keep going'. I went to work, did my job, kept busy at the weekend, and avoided people who looked at me with pity or sympathy. I especially avoided the rescuer types who wanted to have deep and meaningful conversations. I was so afraid that I stayed away from websites, books, pamphlets, and other people's stories about MND. I didn't want to know details. I shopped and read novels, went to films and restaurants. In short, I was on the run. I distracted myself. I didn't even allow myself to cry.

Looking back now when I have learned, to some extent, to be at peace with the road I'm on, I realize I was afraid of losing everything that made up my life, that defined my identity, that gave me a sense of purpose and importance. I liked my job, the busyness and challenges, the relationships and problem-solving. It made me feel important and useful. I didn't want to face a life without having a job, earning money, and being busy in the world. I liked speaking. I liked teaching. I liked laughing with people. I liked the sense that I had life under control, that I had a plan for the next twenty years.

I was afraid of solitude turning into loneliness and depression. I was afraid of helplessness and need, of embarrassment and humiliation when I could no longer look after myself. Other people probably knew it well before I did, but I simply could not speak properly, so how could I be a lecturer at a training college, or a consultant working with teachers? How could I run courses, give feedback, and head up teams? I was so afraid of facing all this.

Finally, hard decisions had to be made and I gave up my job. Some fears were faced, some information read, heard, and accepted about what the future would hold. But the day-to-day living was very hard and raw. I felt I was alone, and I was increasingly silent. I could not answer the phone or explain myself to shopkeepers. I struggled to have coffee with friends because of the effort to speak. I was at home alone for many hours. Fatigue forced me to stop. Everyone else went back to their daily life, everyone but me.

Things changed over time. I got used to my own company, I got used to silence. I developed flashcards for shopping and notebooks to scribble in to explain what I wanted. But I grew afraid of other things. I began to think it would be easiest to just stay at home. I dreaded the doorbell ringing, I was even afraid of emails, and of everything that involved me in the lives of people who might want me to speak to them.

I recognized the danger in this and made a commitment to

myself to join in various things each week, whether I felt like it or not, but all the time my eyes were averted and my face down to try to keep as invisible as I could. I came late to church and left early to avoid people and chatting. I went to shops where I thought my friends would *not* be, I went to films alone and tried to spend my days avoiding interaction. One day I was caught with a stranger who simply asked my name and I scurried in embarrassment to find my notebook and flashcards. That same day I was invited to a meal that suddenly happened around me. I fled. I was afraid of showing how hard it was to chew and swallow, afraid of spitting, drooling, or coughing my meal everywhere as had happened from time to time. I picked up my bag and ran.

I wrote the following poem in 2009:

Fear

Fear
Took me by the throat today

Shook me till
My bones rattled

Chased me
Relentless and cold
Insidious, mocking
Chased me all day

I could have stood my ground
But I ran
So fear
Grew stronger

I was captured
In the end
Quaking and fallen
Curled on the ground in shame[1]

(Rhonda Watson, 2009)

This experience became a turning point for me. I had to decide between fear and courage, between running and standing my ground. One way led downhill to shadows, the other was hard to do, but led to humility and life.

At that time, I was reading John's Gospel and I was struck by the words: ' . . . I chose you and appointed you to go and bear fruit – fruit that will last.'[2] I had been thinking that all my fruit-bearing was over and now I could rest but now I realized that this path I was on must also have opportunities for fruit-bearing. Being ill did not exempt me from obedience to Jesus, who said to his followers: 'You are my friends if you do what I command . . . This is my command: Love each other.'[3]

Everything began to turn around. I realized I had been totally self-absorbed and proud. It took humility to be seen in public, stumbling over words, drooling and weak. But Jesus' command to me involved me seeking to bear fruit, seeking to love others.

So I began to try and follow the advice of the famous American blind and deaf educator, Helen Keller:

> Never bend your head. Always hold it high.
> Look the world straight in the eye.[4]

I began to try to live with courage. Fear began to lose its grip. It's not only me who has this choice. Often, fear dogs us in the daily grind of life and relationships, even when we seem to be just fine. You don't have to have MND to struggle with fear, and to need help to be courageous about life.

God's Word says a great deal about fear. God says we should be afraid, and we are *not* to be afraid. It's something of a conundrum.

God is to be feared, simply because he is God – mighty, holy, sovereign, Creator and Judge. Psalm 76 paints an awe-filled picture of God. He is full of wrath; his name is great; he is resplendent with light; more majestic than mountains; he rebukes and controls the affairs of humans; pronounces judgment from heaven; strikes fear into the land; breaks the spirits of rulers; causes fear in the hearts of kings. Verse 7 expresses it this way: 'You alone are to be feared. Who can stand before you when you are angry?'

In the Old Testament story of God's people, there are some memorable times when God's awesomeness is on display. This display brings a response of fear, and rightly so. Remember the Exodus: the sheer horror of all the first-born Egyptian males dying in one night; the shrill cries of horses and men as chariots were buried under roaring waves when the Red Sea fell back into place; the sight and sound of Mount Sinai covered in thunder, lightning, fire and smoke; the trumpet blasts and earth-quake that heralded God's presence and his word.[5]

There's wisdom in fearing God. It's the place to start if you want to get a right view of yourself and the world and how it all works.

> The fear of the LORD is the beginning of wisdom;
>> all who follow his precepts have good understanding.
>>> (Psalm 111:10)

This kind of fear is due respect for who God is, and it goes hand in hand with worship. Without that fear and recognition of who God is, worship doesn't seem necessary, or it is misguided and false. Paradoxically, this right fear of God leads to peace.

> Whilst fear is a pervasive force within this world, the peace of God or Christ, which stems from due fear or reverence of God, is its most potent adversary, banishing fear.[6]

In a broken world set against God, there is much to fear. The world is not a safe place. It is now filled with sin, hard work, unpredictable events, and marred relationships. Creation, including humanity, is groaning in travail, and swelling in expectancy of the deliverance that is coming. Fear is part of the groaning.

> We know that the whole creation has been groaning as in the pains of childbirth right up to the present time. Not only so, but we ourselves, who have the firstfruits of the Spirit, groan inwardly as we wait eagerly for our adoption as sons, the redemption of our bodies. For in this hope we were saved.
>
> (Romans 8:22–24)

We fear the world which may overwhelm us with fire, flood, earthquake, and uncontrollable events. We fear the 'accidents' of life: the unexpected turn of events like a medical diagnosis, a falling tree, car brakes that fail, a virus, a stumble, a moment's loss of watchfulness.

We fear one another. We carry wounds of childhood, mistakes in our youth, and families that are ill at ease with one another. We carry disappointments and hurts and scars inflicted on us by others. We know the shadowy memories of hurts we have caused *to* others. We know there are relationships in which we failed. We can be weighed down by fear whenever we stop long enough to think and feel.

We fear ourselves, if we are at all honest. We know that we are capable of terrible things, prompted by envy, pride, lust, greed, and bitterness.

We fear the future. We fear what may happen to us, or to those we love. 'What ifs' fill our thoughts – failure at a job, embarrassment in front of others, loss of health or money, loss of approval and, finally, death.

We find that we are wounded by the past, anxious in the present and fearful of the future. Fear seems to be as natural as breathing. So, it is no wonder that there are so many commands not to be afraid. God *commands* us not to be afraid. God doesn't say: 'Look, it's natural to be afraid, I realize that you've had a rough time. Here's a bit of advice from me: it might help if you work at settling your fear. Give it a go and see if you feel a bit better.' No, God says, over and over again, 'Do not be afraid.'[7] How is it possible to obey this instruction not to be afraid? Fear needs to be replaced by something else.

David is honest about his fear and expresses how fear can twist and control us:

> My heart is in anguish within me;
>   the terrors of death assail me.
> Fear and trembling have beset me;
>   horror has overwhelmed me.
>
> (Psalm 55:4–5)

But he also knows to seek to quench his fear with trust in God:

> When I am afraid,
>   I will trust in you.

In God, whose word I praise,
    in God I trust; I will not be afraid.

                                             (Psalm 56:3–4)

Trust in God would be a flimsy replacement for fear without a strong knowledge of who God is and what he is like. The following verses paint a picture of the richness of who God is and why trust in him is such a powerful antidote to fear:

'But you, O Israel, my servant,
    Jacob, whom I have chosen,
    you descendants of Abraham my friend,
I took you from the ends of the earth,
    from its farthest corners I called you.
I said, "You are my servant";
    I have chosen you and have not rejected you.
So do not fear, for I am with you;
    do not be dismayed, for I am your God.

I will strengthen you and help you;

I will uphold you with my righteous right hand.'

(Isaiah 41:8–10)

There is so much packed into these verses. My identity as God's child is rooted in my heritage as descendant of Abraham, child of the covenant. I have been chosen, called, accepted, and given an identity. I enjoy God's presence, my status as his child is secure, and he is committed to help, strengthen, and uphold me. God – Sovereign Redeemer, covenant-keeper, faithful, and compassionate – is *with* me.

Fear nibbles away at us, and we have a daily choice. Do we stoke our fear, or settle it?[8] Do we exercise trust and throw ourselves on our loving Father, asking for strength and help, or do we gnaw away at our fear, like a dog with a rotting bone?

Through Jesus, we can come to God's throne with confidence,

not fear. At this throne we can seek and receive mercy and grace during times of trouble and fear.

> Therefore, since we have a great high priest who has gone through the heavens, Jesus the Son of God, let us hold firmly to the faith we profess. For we do not have a high priest who is unable to sympathise with our weaknesses, but we have one who has been tempted in every way, just as we are – yet was without sin. Let us then approach the throne of grace with confidence, so that we may receive mercy and find grace to help us in our time of need.
>
> (Hebrews 4:14–16)

St Augustine says it so simply. Trust banishes fear.

> Trust the past to God's mercy,
> The present to God's love,
> And the future to God's providence.[9]
>
> (St Augustine)

Alongside trust, a sense of God's greatness is needed. I need to remember who it is I am trusting; like one of the most 'ordinary' of God's creatures, the simple marsh hen.

> As the marsh hen secretly builds on the watery sod,
> Behold I will build me a nest on the greatness of God;
> I will fly in the greatness of God as the marsh hen flies
> In the freedom that fills all the space 'twixt the marsh and
> the skies:
> By so many roots as the marsh-grass sends in the sod
> I will heartily lay me a-hold on the greatness of God.[10]
>
> Sidney Lanier (1842–1881)

So as I face the future I will seek to be real about my fears, but not ruled by them; I will put my trust in God who is both powerful and loving; I will look back to the stories of God's faithfulness and forward to his ongoing providence. I will make my nest in him.

O God, our help in ages past
O God, our help in ages past,
Our hope for years to come,
Our shelter from the stormy blast,
And our eternal home.

Under the shadow of Thy throne
Thy saints have dwelt secure,
Sufficient is Thine arm alone,
And our defence is sure.

Before the hills in order stood,
Or earth received her frame,
From everlasting Thou art God,
To endless years the same.

A thousand ages in Thy sight
Are like an evening gone,
Short as the watch that ends the night
Before the rising sun.

Time, like an ever-rolling stream,
Bears all its sons away;
They fly forgotten, as a dream
Dies at the opening day.

O God, our help in ages past,
Our hope for years to come,
Be thou our guard while troubles last,
And our eternal home.[11]

(Isaac Watts, 1674–1748)

Prayer

O Lord, let me lay hold of your greatness, your compassion, your trustworthiness. Let my vision of you banish my daily fears. Jesus, my brother, high priest and Lord, I come in your name to the throne of God; please give me grace and strength. Holy Spirit, counsellor and friend, keep my eyes on Jesus and what he has done for me, keep my heart warm with hope for his coming, and empower me to live for God's glory.

Remember …

Our mighty and loving God says to us: 'Do not be afraid. Trust me.'

Be honest about fear and pride.

Commit yourself to live with courage.

Strengthen courage because of who God is: mighty, sovereign, saving Lord.

Strengthen courage because of who we are: God's loved children,
under his care.

Seek to banish fear with deepening trust in God.

Reflect

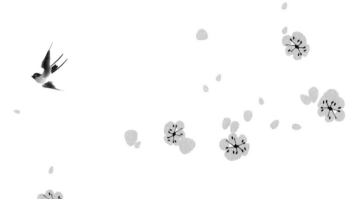

four

Thankfulness and bitterness

Thankfulness demands
an open face to God,
a stance of trust
and delight.

As the days and months pass with this chronic disease, the challenge has become entirely different. At first there was shock, horror, fear, anger, and many strong thoughts and feelings to deal with. After time passed and the disease made slow but insidious 'progress', life became difficult in other ways. The daily mundane chore of living, passing the time, being alone, and being silent threatened me with apathy and a sense of meaninglessness.

Now the challenge that presents itself for me, and others who feel trapped by their circumstances, is how to live a rich, full, worthwhile life in this difficult context.

My friend Glenn sent me an email soon after my diagnosis forced me to stop work. It struck me then and I re-read it often. So many people were sending me cards and emails full of sadness and sympathy; his stood out because it was so different. He said:

> May God's strength be your inner strength as you address this
> debilitating disease, knowing that in the end the Lord's name
> will be exalted – and he has chosen you to exalt his name in
> this particular way at this particular time, for his glory.

This email, sent off to support and encourage me, struck me with
its bold message. This was no sentimental sympathy message,
warm and schmaltzy; this was a strong call to stand up and seek
to glorify God in the middle of MND. It wasn't about me, it was
about exalting God. It was a healthy reminder.

The prominent early-twentieth-century minister and teacher,
Oswald Chambers, captures the same challenge, and it's not just
for people with a disabling disease, or a great sorrow to bear,
it's for most of us on most days when the simple daily routine is
tough going.

> It does require the supernatural grace of God to live twenty-
> four hours in every day as a saint, to go through drudgery as

a disciple, to live an ordinary, unobserved, ignored existence as a disciple of Jesus. It is inbred in us that we have to do exceptional things for God; but we have not. We have to be exceptional in the ordinary things, to be holy in mean streets, among mean people, and this is not learned in five minutes.[1]

(Oswald Chambers)

'To live an ordinary, unobserved, ignored existence as a disciple of Jesus . . . ' This expresses the challenge for a great many disciples. I am not 'special' in needing to live this way. How many people are at home with children and babies living 'unobserved' lives? How many are sick or living alone? How many people are forced into a job that is mundane and boring and apparently unimportant? How many have missed out on opportunities to use their creativity? How many are trapped in difficult loveless relationships? The list goes on, and we haven't even considered those imprisoned or rejected by family, or in poverty in the persecuted church around the world. There are many who face the challenge to 'live an ordinary, unobserved, ignored existence as a disciple of Jesus'.

This is 'everyday theology', the sense that ordinary everyday people and our everyday contexts are where we display what our theology really means. It is where belief meets daily habit. It's all about life – real life, daily tasks, drudgery, and routine, being just as significant as the great noteworthy and public moments. It's trying to apply Abraham Kuyper's 'every square inch' catchcry. He said, when explaining the significance of the Lordship of Christ:

> There is not a square inch in the whole domain of our human existence over which Christ, who is sovereign over all, does not cry: 'Mine!'[2]
>
> (Abraham Kuyper)

Well then, if I really believe in the Lordship of Christ over every square inch, including me here and now, with MND and all my growing limitations, I had best work out what his cry of 'Mine!'

means right now, right here, for me. You, in your own situation, will need to grapple with this same question.

As I thought about how I might respond to Jesus' Lordship over my present situation, I became convinced of the need to develop an attitude of thankfulness. What was my alternative? The absence of thankfulness is bitterness, resentment, self-pity and despair.

Bitterness can be a natural response to life's trials. Job, in his bewilderment at the tragic events that befell him, cried out to God:

> 'Therefore I will not keep silent;
>   I will speak out in the anguish of my spirit,
>   I will complain in the bitterness of my soul.'

> (Job 7:11)

Naomi is another Old Testament example, who is so overwhelmed with grief that she changes her name to 'bitterness'. She despairs at what God has brought to her.

'Don't call me Naomi,' she told them. 'Call me Mara, because the Almighty has made my life very bitter. I went away full, but the Lord has brought me back empty. Why call me Naomi? The Lord has afflicted me; the Almighty has brought misfortune upon me.'

(Ruth 1:20–21)

By the end of the narrative in Ruth, Naomi once again experiences joy and hope. It took changed circumstances for Naomi to trust God again and praise him. A far greater challenge is to trust and worship God, even when the circumstances do not change, or indeed, if they become steadily worse.

Naomi's response of bitterness came from her sense of God being untrustworthy. She experienced tragedy and she said, 'Look what God has done to me! I give in to my despair.' Job takes a slightly more aggressive stance; it's more like, 'Hey, God! This is wrong. It's *not* OK what's happened to me. Come on, give me a good reason!' This kind of reactive anger and bitterness is understandable from Job as he struggles to deal with all that has happened to him. Both responses are of people struggling with their unbelief. Both responses reflect people who are wondering if God is impotent, uncaring, and unwilling; or incompetent, foolish, and fickle. This struggle can lead to a long-term hardness and bitterness that springs from unbelief, or a mistaken understanding of God's nature and his purposes. In Job's case, he finally came to a place of acceptance before God, a realization of God's sovereignty and his own human limitations.

I have always loved Psalm 62 and have returned to it often over the years when life has been difficult to endure or understand. Verses 11 to 12 describe two characteristics of God which I need to hold together, especially during times of grief and bewilderment:

One thing God has spoken,
two things have I heard:

that you, O God, are strong,

    and that you, O Lord, are loving.

                                  (Psalm 62:11–12)

The challenge for us, when circumstances are painful, when hope is hard to find, and when things just keep getting worse, is to reject unbelief and despair. Why? Because God *is* strong, and God *is* loving. He is both sovereign and committed to us because he loves us. This is true, even if we can't see or feel it to be true.

When bitterness creeps into the kingdom community, it is to be dealt with and we are to get rid of it. It is to be replaced with kindness, compassion, and forgiveness.[3] If there is no place for bitterness in the community of God's people, then there ought to be no place for bitterness at a personal level.

Bitterness may not always be a strong emotion or an extreme response. I don't usually cry out with demands like Job, or in complete despair, like Naomi. However, I do accept sinister 'little' emotions like irritable self-centredness, cooling of my trust in God, silent envy of others, and sulking. Somehow I allow this kind of bitterness a foothold, and tell myself I have a right to feel this way. This is still bitterness. I must reject it.

This chapter was begun weeks ago. It turned out to be harder to write than I expected. Why? Well, I may not feel full of strong bitterness, but I am truly struggling to be deeply and authentic-ally thankful. I don't like this slow decline, solitude, and silence; nor this loneliness, diminishing of my identity and my relation-ships. I am weary of trying to 'stay positive' and cheerful. I'm grumbling, I'm discouraged, I'm retreating. Thankfulness demands an open face to God, a stance of trust and delight. I'm finding that a difficult thing right now, but it's crucial for my survival. I must develop thankfulness as a habit and a commitment. I find the following statement by the apostle Paul to be frighteningly difficult to imitate, but more crucial than ever before:

> Therefore I will boast all the more gladly about my weaknesses, so that Christ's power may rest on me. That is why, for Christ's sake, I delight in weaknesses, in insults, in hardships, in persecutions, in difficulties. For when I am weak, then I am strong.
>
> (2 Corinthians 12:9–10)

Here's my personal challenge: to delight in my weaknesses for the sake of Christ being exalted; to accept the gnawing changes in my brain and body as an opportunity for Christ's power to be made obvious; to trust in the God who is both strong and loving; and to be thankful.

Recently I saw and heard Verdi's Requiem. How glorious it was! As I walked down the steps of Sydney Opera House, I was full of thankfulness, because I had the money to buy the tickets, the hearing to absorb the glorious sound, the strength to get into my seat and someone to drive me there and back. The harbour glistened with spring sunshine and the coffee tasted good. In that moment, thankfulness came easily. My thankfulness matters to God, and it may matter all the more if it is hard to conjure up, if it springs from the grey days. 'A wounded deer leaps highest' wrote the nineteenth-century American poet, Emily Dickinson. The widow's tiny offering was pleasing to Jesus, for out of her poverty she gave all she had.[4] My thankfulness has to be dragged out of me sometimes, for I often feel poverty-stricken, weak, and barely able to turn to God in trust. In those moments, my tiny offering of thankfulness is deeply pleasing to Jesus, for it is all I have to give.

So my thankfulness, and yours, in the face of the pain and wounds we feel, will spring all the higher in exalting Christ. Christ, who declares, 'Mine!' over us, our situation, our struggle, and our sadness, will be exalted and honoured by our thankfulness. Like a breath of cool sea breeze, thankfulness clears away bitter grumbling, self-pity, and hardness of heart.

Thankfulness matters to God. He even legislated for it, requiring a thanksgiving offering of the people of Israel.[5] In the Psalms, thanksgiving becomes an outpouring of worship, both corporate and personal. In Psalm 95, the community comes before God with thanksgiving and joy which is founded on who he is – the Lord, the rock of salvation, the great God, the King above all, sovereign over creation – and who they are in relation to him – creatures, people under his care.

Come, let us sing for joy to the LORD;
    let us shout aloud to the Rock of our salvation.
Let us come before him with thanksgiving
    and extol him with music and song.

For the LORD is the great God,
    the great King above all gods.
In his hand are the depths of the earth,
    and the mountain peaks belong to him.

The sea is his, for he made it,
　　and his hands formed the dry land.

Come, let us bow down in worship,
　　let us kneel before the Lᴏʀᴅ our Maker;
for he is our God
　　and we are the people of his pasture,
　　the flock under his care.

(Psalm 95:1–7)

Psalm 147 is more personal. In this psalm, God is described as the one who binds up the broken-hearted, brings healing and sustains the humble. Though he is almighty Lord of all, he takes delight in the one who fears him and trusts in his love. The call of this psalm is to sing to the Lord with thanksgiving and, the amazing thing is, this brings God delight. In this psalm, it is not the able-bodied who bring God delight but those who offer him thankfulness, respect, and who hope in his unfailing love. That much I can do; and it is no small thing to God, the sovereign creator of all.

Praise the LORD.

How good it is to sing praises to our God,
how pleasant and fitting to praise him!

The LORD builds up Jerusalem;
he gathers the exiles of Israel.
He heals the broken-hearted
and binds up their wounds.
He determines the number of the stars
and calls them each by name.
Great is our Lord and mighty in power;
his understanding has no limit.
The LORD sustains the humble
but casts the wicked to the ground.

Sing to the LORD with thanksgiving;
make music to our God on the harp.

He covers the sky with clouds;
    he supplies the earth with rain
    and makes grass grow on the hills.
He provides food for the cattle
    and for the young ravens when they call.

His pleasure is not in the strength of the horse,
    nor his delight in the legs of a man;
the Lord delights in those who fear him,
    who put their hope in his unfailing love.

(Psalm 147:1–11)

Followers of Jesus have even richer truths to draw upon in developing the habit of thankfulness. In Jesus we have Lord and Saviour, Brother and King, high priest and sacrifice. We have promises of resurrection to come, evidence of a risen saviour, and God's Spirit to empower us. How much more to be thankful for! No longer in need of a law that requires us to bring thank offerings, we live by the Spirit who pours out God's love into our hearts, comforting and strengthening us, and drawing from us the response of thankfulness and trust.[6] God invites us to come to him with thanksgiving when we bring our needs and cares to him.

> Do not be anxious about anything, but in everything, by prayer and petition, with thanksgiving, present your requests to God. And the peace of God, which transcends all understanding, will guard your hearts and your minds in Christ Jesus.
>
> (Philippians 4:6–7)

Our thankfulness is to be overflowing and abundant. It is an integral part of spiritual growth and maturity.

> So then, just as you received Christ Jesus as Lord, continue to live in him, rooted and built up in him, strengthened in the faith as you were taught, and overflowing with thankfulness.
>
> (Colossians 2:6–7)

None of this comes easily. It didn't come easily to Paul. His life was full of both wonderful and devastating experiences. He carried the treasure of the gospel, the indwelling of the Holy Spirit, in a faulty container: himself. His description resonates with me – hard pressed, perplexed, persecuted, struck down, given over to death.

> But we have this treasure in jars of clay to show that this all-surpassing power is from God and not from us. We are hard pressed on every side, but not crushed; perplexed, but not in despair; persecuted, but not abandoned; struck down, but not destroyed. We always carry around in our body the death of Jesus, so that the life of Jesus may also be revealed in our body. For we who are alive are always being given over to death for Jesus' sake, so that his life may be revealed in our mortal body . . . All this is for your benefit, so that the grace that is reaching more and more people may cause thanksgiving to overflow to the glory of God.
>
> (2 Corinthians 4:7–11, 15)

Alongside the pressure is God's provision: not crushed, not in despair, not abandoned, not destroyed, but revealing the life and power of Jesus. And what is the underlying purpose and outcome of Paul's struggles? That thanksgiving may overflow, to the glory of God.

Thankfulness places me in the role of receiver, and acknowledges God as sovereign and gracious giver. In times of strength and health, I hardly ever think of myself as the passive receiver of God's good gifts. I'm too busy, too active, too self-important. Neediness reverses all that, and I come more readily with open hands to God the giver.

Thankfulness emphasizes my 'receiver-ship'. It acknowledges good gifts. The everyday good gifts of God are often overlooked – good coffee, comfortable shoes, autumn colours, scampering dogs, clean water, an email from a friend. In receiving gifts with thankfulness we honour the giver. All of this brings a stance of dignity and courage. A friend once told me, 'Self-pity is very unattractive.' Thankfulness then, is beautiful.

I need God to draw this attitude from me. On my darkest days I will not find thankfulness near at hand. Graham Kendrick expresses this need in his beautiful prayer and song, 'Lord, you've been good to me':

Lord, you've been good to me
Lord, you've been good to me
All my life, all my life;
Your loving-kindness never fails.
I will remember
All you have done,
Bring from my heart
Thanksgiving songs.

New every morning is your love,
Filled with compassion from above.

Grace and forgiveness full and free,
Lord, you've been good to me.

So may each breath I take
Be for you, only you,
Giving you back the life I owe.
Love so amazing,
Mercy so free.
Lord, you've been good,
So good to me.[7]

(Graham Kendrick, 2001)

Thankfulness quells self-pity. It stops a hankering after 'the good old days', the time before all this happened. The times when I could . . . , when I had . . . , when I was known for . . . . The habit of thankfulness stops the habit of envy: I wish I had what she's got, I wish I could do what he does, I wish, I wish, I want, I want. Thankfulness forces me to let go of all that.

Thankfulness enables me to live in the moment. It accepts the present and looks for and enjoys what is tasty, pleasant, fresh, good, and warm. It takes my focus away from myself and allows me to see the needs and feelings of others.

The old hymn, 'Now thank we all our God', captures the attitude of thankfulness so well. It was first sung in Germany in the 1600s and has been offered to God as a prayer by generations of Christians ever since:

Now thank we all our God
Now thank we all our God,
With hearts and hands and voices;
Who wondrous things hath done,
In whom his world rejoices;
Who, from our mother's arms
Hath blessed us on our way
With countless gifts of love,
And still is ours today.

O may this bounteous God
Through all our life be near us,
With ever-joyful hearts
And blessed peace to cheer us;
And keep us in his grace,
And guide us when perplexed,
And free us from all ills
In this world and the next.

All praise and thanks to God
The Father now be given,
The Son, and Him who reigns
With them in highest heaven,
The one, eternal God,
Whom earth and heaven adore;
For thus it was, is now,
And shall be evermore.[8]

(Martin Rinkart, 1586–1649, tr. Catherine Winkworth)

Prayer

Lord God, teach me thankfulness.

Remember ...

Thankfulness springs from a deep awareness of God's generous grace. It lifts our hearts and brings God delight.

Be a faithful follower of Jesus in the ordinary things of life, even if God alone can see us.

Develop a habit of thankfulness and an awareness of God's generosity each day.

Express your feelings to God honestly and openly, but don't allow a settled sense of bitterness.

Be thankful, even in the dark and difficult times, knowing it brings honour to God.

By being thankful, avoid self-pity.

Reflect

five

Joy and grief

Acceptance of
grief is part
of the journey
towards joy.

Sometimes the longing for joy is elusive and mysterious. During the writing of this chapter I have experienced days of terrible sadness and darkness, which is no surprise really. Yet, I am told in the Bible to rejoice. Even more bewildering is the command to 'Consider it pure joy . . . whenever you face trials of many kinds'.[1] Sometimes this sounds absurd. However I may struggle to grasp joy, I certainly know the longing for it very well. Joy is big, strong, captivating, and deep. The following poem, 'Joy' by the American writer, Carl Sandburg, communicates it well I think.

Joy

Let a joy keep you.
Reach out your hands
And take it when it runs by,
As the Apache dancer
Clutches his woman.
I have seen them
Live long and laugh loud,

Sent on singing, singing,
Smashed to the heart
Under the ribs
With a terrible love.
Joy always,
Joy everywhere –
Let joy kill you!
Keep away from the little deaths.[2]

(Carl Sandburg, 1878–1967)

We recognize it with a stab of longing when we see joy in others. We know that joy can feel strong and untamed, and we long for the 'smashed to the heart' feeling it gives us. We know that joy can sweep us up in a torrent yet we would rather be 'killed' by it than die many small and meaningless deaths.

We can deny ourselves the possibility of joy, if we also run from the other emotions of life. How can we really be joyful if we deny our grief? There seems to be a need to be real with ourselves at an emotional level, and to resist the habits that we use to distract ourselves from feeling. To be fully and deeply human involves full and deep emotion.

Jesus is our example in this. He experienced the full range of emotions, faced them and felt them, and continued to trust and obey his Father. Picture him at Lazarus' grave, weeping with deep feeling;[3] see him filled with compassion and longing as he looks over Jerusalem, crying, 'O Jerusalem, Jerusalem';[4] remember him as he gently raises the son of a widow, filled with compassion for her;[5] and recall his sorrow as the rich young man walked away, because 'Jesus looked at him and loved him'.[6] Jesus experienced fully the emotions of being human.

I love this poem by the British-born American poet, Denise Levertov, because it reminds me to make peace with my emotions, including my grief. Keep one emotion at arm's length and they all seem to be distant.

Talking to Grief

Ah, Grief, I should not treat you
like a homeless dog
who comes to the back door
for a crust, for a meatless bone.
I should trust you.

I should coax you
into the house and give you
your own corner,
a worn mat to lie on,
your own water dish.

You think I don't know you've been living
under my porch.
You long for your real place to be readied
before winter comes. You need
your name,
your collar and tag. You need

the right to warn off intruders,
to consider
my house your own
and me your person
and yourself
my own dog[7]

(Denise Levertov, 1923–1997)

I need to face and even embrace my grief and sorrow on my way to joy and comfort. Levertov acknowledges the need to accept what is causing her grief, to welcome it, name it and put it to bed. Acceptance of grief is part of the journey towards joy. While we busy ourselves with distraction and denial, fleeing our hurts, we may also hold joy at arm's length.

The Psalms give expression to the full range of human emotions. Why do we love the Psalms so much? I think one reason is because of their daring. They dare to give honest expression to our strongest emotions. They say things we feel we are 'not allowed to say' out loud. They throw caution to the wind, expressing anger, fear, dismay, depression, outrage, love, bewilderment, grief, hunger, yearning, confusion – and joy.

For a Christian, there's no choice about joy. It is commanded. However, it hasn't always been a characteristic of my life. I have had to learn it late in life.

> Shout with joy to God, all the earth!
>> Sing the glory of his name;
>> make his praise glorious!

(Psalm 66:1–2)

Now, in my mature years, how I wish I was better at joy. I look at the way some Christians flinch from music that stirs emotions. I hear the shallowness of our prayers and the way we avoid 'pouring out our hearts'. Our restraint seems to have made us weak, not strong; our self-control tends to make us aloof; and our correctness has made us, well, correct. I am as much a part of this as anyone. As I reach the tail end of my life, I long to embrace joy more wholeheartedly.

Over and over, God commands his people to be joyful. That itself is strange. How can I be *made* to be joyful? It seems joy matters deeply to God, but his people are so bad at it that he has to keep telling them they must do it. The Old Testament Law included a feast lasting seven days, full of eating and drinking and rejoicing before the Lord.[8] The people were to rejoice in their work, enjoy the harvest, and eat their tithes![9] Those who could not make it to the meeting place were told to sell their tithes and use the silver to 'buy anything you wish'[10] and rejoice before God. One aspect of God's judgment on his people was their failure to serve him with joy:

> Because you did not serve the LORD your God joyfully and gladly in the time of prosperity, therefore in hunger and thirst, in nakedness and dire poverty, you will serve the enemies the LORD sends against you.
>
> (Deuteronomy 28:47–48)

The rest of creation responds with rejoicing before God. There is rejoicing because God is sovereign; there is rejoicing at the sheer brilliance and wonder of God's creativity; there is rejoicing at the display of God's love and redemption of his people.

Let the heavens rejoice, let the earth be glad;
    let them say among the nations, 'The Lord reigns!'

(1 Chronicles 16:31)

Then the Lord answered Job out of the storm. He said:

'Where were you when I laid the earth's foundation? . . .
while the morning stars sang together
    and all the angels shouted for joy?'

(Job 38:1, 4, 7)

Sing for joy, O heavens, for the Lord has done this;
    shout aloud, O earth beneath.

> Burst into song, you mountains,
>> you forests and all your trees,
> for the LORD has redeemed Jacob,
>> he displays his glory in Israel.

(Isaiah 44:23)

It often seems that life robs us of the possibility of joy. How can we rejoice at such times? I have watched others in the midst of terrible loss and despair, determined to go on trusting, go on rejoicing in God. In the face of inexplicable suffering, knowing it comes under God's sovereignty and feeling broken-hearted, we can still determine to rejoice. Habakkuk saw visions of terrible things that were to unfold for God's people. He was filled with fear: 'I heard and my heart pounded, my lips quivered at the sound; decay crept into my bones, and my legs trembled.'[11] When I hear about what lies ahead of me with MND, I feel much the same way! And yet, and yet . . . in Habakkuk's words:

Though the fig-tree does not bud
    and there are no grapes on the vines,
though the olive crop fails
    and the fields produce no food,
though there are no sheep in the pen
    and no cattle in the stalls,
yet I will rejoice in the LORD,
    I will be joyful in God my Saviour.

(Habakkuk 3:17–18)

How can this kind of response be possible? It is a response of belief: determined, active, thoughtful belief. This is a determination to trust in God, despite everything one sees, feels, fears, and loses. It seems to me that there can be no joy unless one believes that God is sovereign, God is good, God is faithful, and he can be trusted, no matter what.

To trust in the strength of God in our weakness is victory. To say, *I am weak: so let me be. God is strong*, is victory. To seek from him who is our life, as the natural, simple cure of all that is amiss with us, the power to *do*, and *be*, and *live*, even when we are weary – this is the victory that overcomes the world.

To believe in God our strength in the face of all seeming denial . . . to believe in him out of the heart of weakness and unbelief in spite of numbness and weariness and lethargy . . . to believe in the wide-awake *real*, through all the stupefying, enervating, distorting dream . . . to will to wake up when the very being seems athirst for a godless repose – these are the broken steps up to the high fields where repose is but a form of strength, strength but a form of joy, joy but a form of love.[12]

(George MacDonald)

How is it possible to trust in this way? For me, it is all wrapped up in the cross of Jesus. Jesus, God himself dwelling amongst us, sacrificed himself, and entered into dread, grief, suffering, and humiliation. Jesus did this as a response of obedience to his Father; the Father asked it of him out of love for his world.[13] He did it for the joy that was to come.

> Let us fix our eyes on Jesus, the author and perfector of our faith, who for the joy set before him endured the cross, scorning its shame, and sat down at the right hand of the throne of God. Consider him who endured such opposition from sinful men, so that you will not grow weary and lose heart.
>
> (Hebrews 12:2–3)

Jesus' suffering proves to me that he fully understands my own times of darkness and pain. Jesus knows about this awkward dance of grief and joy. He went to the cross to ensure my joy. How can I ever take joy as an optional extra, when it cost him so much to guarantee it for me? So I commit myself to joy. God is also committed to my joy.

Jesus paints a complex and beautiful image of my intimate relationship with him, an intertwining of love, obedience, and joy connected like a Celtic knot:

> As the Father has loved me, so have I loved you. Now remain in my love. If you obey my commands, you will remain in my love, just as I have obeyed my Father's commands and remain in his love. I have told you this so that my joy may be in you and that your joy may be complete.
>
> (John 15:9–11)

In this life, joy may feel fleeting, more like a wave that ebbs and flows than a still, deep lake; it may seem fragile and so breakable.

> All joy (as distinct from mere pleasure, still more amusement) emphasises our pilgrim status; always reminds, beckons, awakens desire. Our best havings are wantings.[14]
>
> (C. S. Lewis)

The future for me, in the new creation, involves the magnificent prospect of thousands upon thousands around the throne, worshipping the Lamb with great joy. On that day I will have my voice again, a new voice, fit to praise God as he deserves, and what joy it will give me to join with people from all the nations and across all the centuries![15] That's what my longing is for, that's what my joy stirs in me.

Meanwhile, I seek to obey the clear command:

> Rejoice in the Lord always. I will say it again: Rejoice!
>
> (Philippians 4:4)

I hope to obey, with confidence that God will give me the strength to do it:

> To him who is able to keep you from falling and to present you before his glorious presence without fault and with great joy – to the only God our Saviour be glory, majesty, power and

authority, through Jesus Christ our Lord, before all ages, now
and for evermore! Amen.

(Jude 1:24–25)

Hymn of Joy

Joyful, joyful we adore thee,
God of glory, Lord of love;
Hearts unfold like flowers before thee,
Praising thee, their sun above.
Melt the clouds of sin and sadness;
Drive the dark of doubt away;
Giver of immortal gladness,
Fill us with the light of day!

All thy works with joy surround thee,
Earth and heaven reflect thy rays,
Stars and angels sing around thee,
Centre of unbroken praise.

Field and forest, vale and mountain,
Blooming meadow, flashing sea,
Chanting bird and flowing fountain
Call us to rejoice in thee.

Thou art giving and forgiving,
Ever blessing, ever blest,
Well-spring of the joy of living,
Ocean-depth of happy rest!
Thou our Father, Christ our Brother,
All who live in love are thine;
Teach us how to love each other,
Lift us to the Joy Divine.

Mortals join the mighty chorus,
Which the morning stars began;
Father-love is reigning o'er us,
Brother-love binds man to man.

Ever singing, march we onward,
Victors in the midst of strife,
Joyful music lifts us sunward
In the triumph song of life.[16]

(Henry van Dyke, 1852–1933)

Prayer

Heavenly Father, you are the source of joy.
You long for my joy, you teach me where to find joy,
and you promise true lasting joy to come.
I lay my grief before you.
I seek healing and lightness when I am heavy and weary.
And I lift my face to see you, Joy itself, Lord Jesus.

Remember ...

Like Jesus, we can be joyful in the midst of sorrow. Like Jesus, we can put our hope in the joy that is to come.

Follow Jesus' example, feeling sorrow
yet still rejoicing.

Be an authentic person in the midst of suffering –
honest about grief and sorrow.

Use the Psalms as expressions of joy, praise,
and longing.

Rejoice in the Lord!

Ask God for his gift of joy.

Reflect

six

Delight and despair

The doctrine of God's providence
brings us joy
and helps us delight in God
in the face of long cold dark days.

On my wall hangs a felt doll. You need to get the right idea about this doll. There are no frills or pink bits of lace. There's not even a smiling face. This is a tough doll. This is a doll created in the cold hills of Kazakhstan. It is made of rough thick felted wool, grown by shepherds in those hills. It is handmade by women – Christian women – who struggle to feed their families and keep warm. The doll has a red dress, legs covered in tough black wool, and a red pointed hat with fur edges. The doll is dressed for the winter cold, and the winter dark. It has a strong face, staring resolutely at me, with no cute smile or fluttering eyelashes. Look more closely and you can see a little piece of swirling hand-sewn embroidery on the dress and a band of bright braid around the neck.

What I love about this doll is the story behind it. There are real women behind this doll, Christians who are determined to find a way to survive and a way to make something gentle and beautiful in the midst of their struggles. I hope one day, in the new creation, to meet the woman who made this doll and thank her for the encouragement she has brought me. I need a tough doll on my wall for days when chronic illness leaves me struggling with despair.

Despair is something we all taste because this world serves us up ladles of disappointment, hurt, and sorrow. Despair can overwhelm us and we can become pulled down and down into the mud until we fold up and die. We may be sitting up in bed, lying on a couch, or hobbling down the road, but inside there is a heavy sense of surrender – that is the road despair takes us on.

In Australia we experience extremes in climate cycles. Recently we have had months of rain and it has brought the country to life. For the first time in many years, the huge inland lake in the middle of the desert, Lake Eyre, has filled with water. Up from the sand have come frogs and water creatures which lay buried for years, waiting for moisture. Tens of thousands of birds arrived at the new lake to breed. It is a total transformation from desert to watery oasis.

However, there have been long years of drought leading to this. Farmers lost their crops year after year. They sowed seed in hope that rain would come and it didn't. The price of lamb has sky-rocketed as farmers had sold off everything in previous years rather than see their stock die in the dry paddocks. In those long years of drought, suicide became the way out for many farmers who could no longer find the strength to wait for rain as their debts piled up higher and higher. The taste of despair lay heavy on country Australia.

While we know that despair is a bad road to choose, it can be very difficult to choose differently. What other roads are available? How can we resist despair? The psalmist explains his experience:

> If your law had not been my delight,
>   I would have perished in my affliction.

(Psalm 119:92)

For the psalmist, delight was the antidote to despair, it stopped him perishing in the midst of his experience of suffering. I find this a helpful image; that delight is a weapon, a way to ward off despair. Often we look for happy moments, times in the sun, special treats, and experiences to delight in. We learn from this psalm that choosing delight in God's Word can be a deep stabilizing choice despite the circumstances we face. The psalmist took deliberate determined delight in God's Word and it saved him from being overwhelmed with his suffering.

David focuses our thinking further when he says:

Delight yourself in the LORD
   and he will give you the desires of your heart.

Commit your way to the LORD;
   trust in him and he will do this:
He will make your righteousness shine like the dawn . . .

                        (Psalm 37:4–6)

David said these words when he was being threatened by evil men who were plotting against him, seeking his downfall. He stopped, took a breath and reminded himself: 'Delight yourself in the Lord!' What was the result? For David it meant the desires of his heart aligned with his delight in God, and he trusted God to fulfil those desires. It meant active committing of his way to God, resolute trusting in God. The result was not a sudden disappearance of all his troubles, but rather his righteousness shining in full view.

Do you have times when you ask yourself, and God: What is my life worth right now? I'm not productive, I accept help but am rarely able to give it, I can't use all the talents you gave me, I have withdrawn from daily life. What's my purpose in being alive?

Those are understandable questions and it is natural to ask them. What happens next is what matters. You have two choices for how you think and act. *Choice 1*: I am worthless, I don't know why God would inflict this useless suffering on me, I give up, I will turn my face to the wall and surrender to these feelings in despair. *Choice 2*: This is tough going, it's hard to hold on to a sense of worth, but nevertheless I will commit my way to God, I will attune my desires to his ways, I will trust him, and I will seek to delight in him.

Maybe no one but God and a handful of others can see our choice, nevertheless, we can choose this way of trust. For me, on a sunny spring day in Australia surrounded by warmth, flowers, baby birds, and towering white gumtrees, I glance over at the doll from Kazakhstan and remember the women there heading into another tough winter of cold and persecution. And for this moment, this day, I choose to reject despair. And there it is: my moment of choice.

Delight can be close at hand. One positive outcome of sickness and disability can be learning to see what's near at hand and to value it. Seneca, the writer from ancient times, said:

> Is it so small a thing to have enjoyed the sun, to have lived
> light in the Spring, to have loved, to have thought, to have
> done, to have advanced true friends?
>
> (Seneca)

This is such a needful antidote to a society that tends to race through each day, lives to buy and possess, and seeks to be entertained by distractions and experiences. Delight can be near at hand and accessible, and grounded in everyday things and people, if we have eyes to see and willingness to welcome it.

This way of thinking about delight turns our eyes towards God and his sovereign providence. Personally, this focus is critical for my daily survival and my daily rejection of despair. God is sovereign; he rules the details of my life in his mercy and goodness.

> Ignorance of providence is the greatest of all miseries, and the
> knowledge of it the highest happiness.
>
> (John Calvin)

The doctrine of God's providence may sound old-fashioned, or a hangover from the Puritans, but this belief is foundational to biblical Christianity. It is God's governing and preserving of his creation carried out in wisdom, power, and mercy. Through his providence, God keeps creation alive, is actively involved in his world, and directs everything towards the fulfilment of his purposes. To make God's providence personal: God keeps me alive each day, he is actively involved in my daily experiences, and he is purposefully directing my circumstances and my health to fulfil his purposes for me.

> All the days ordained for me
> were written in your book
> before one of them came to be.
>
> (Psalm 139:16)

Are not two sparrows sold for a penny? Yet not one of them will fall to the ground apart from the will of your Father. And even the very hairs of your head are all numbered. So don't be afraid; you are worth more than many sparrows.

(Matthew 10:29–31)

There is a mystery here that means we need to hold together complementary truths.

> A person takes action, or an event is triggered by natural causes, or Satan shows his hand – yet God overrules . . . Things that are done contravene God's will of command – yet they fulfil his will of events . . . Humans mean what they do for evil – yet God overrules and uses their actions for good.[1]
>
> (J. I. Packer)

The doctrine of providence brings us joy and helps us delight in God in the face of long cold dark days. It means we are never in the grip of meaningless events and hidden forces. It means that all that happens to us happens by God's hand. As each challenge comes to us, it comes as a call from God to trust him, delight in him, and keep on obeying him. It means that our struggles, although they feel full of dread and hopelessness, are really for our spiritual and eternal good.

This mighty, sovereign, providential God is our Heavenly Father. When Jesus' disciples saw him at prayer, they instinctively knew their inadequacy and pleaded: 'Lord, teach us to pray'.[2] He answered by turning their attention to God their Father. Jesus said such freeing and encouraging words, especially for those of us who are weak and ill. He said that prayer is between you and God, it only needs to be direct and simple, and God your Father knows what you need even before you ask him.[3]

'This, then, is how you should pray:

"Our Father in heaven,
    hallowed be your name,
your kingdom come,

your will be done
   on earth as it is in heaven.
Give us today our daily bread.
Forgive us our debts,
   as we have also forgiven our debtors.
And lead us not into temptation,
   but deliver us from the evil one."'

(Matthew 6:9–13)

I turn to look at Jesus and see God the Son struggling against despair, deliberately choosing trust and obedience, even in the face of his sense of dread. Remember Jesus in Gethsemane just hours before his arrest. He says to his bewildered friends: 'My soul is overwhelmed with sorrow to the point of death. Stay here and keep watch with me.'[4] Then Jesus pours out his soul to his Father, and struggles against despair and overwhelming sorrow. He struggles towards trust and obedience. This is our Saviour, a man who has experienced dark days of struggle. This sight of Jesus at prayer in Gethsemane warms my heart and encourages me to pray. There he is, tasting terrible anguish; so I know he understands my days of anguish.

In my struggle with days of despair I also need to remember that it is God's power to hold on to me that really matters. As I read the Gospels these days I so readily identify with the poor, sick, needy, and troubled who came to Jesus for help. That's me on the mat being lowered through the roof; there I am at the edges of the crowd reaching out to touch the hem of Jesus' robe as he passes; I am the woman hobbling into the synagogue, bent over and deformed. All I bring is my need and weakness. I never understood before how simple it is. Now I do. I am in need; I come to Jesus for help.

My own hands grow weaker and I find I keep dropping things. My muscles twitch and the neurons misfire down my nerve endings. I drop my food, dribble when I eat, and can't perform some of the simplest tasks. My grip on my physical world is slipping. But I have a Saviour whose grip on me is unbreakable.

> My sheep listen to my voice; I know them, and they follow me.
> I give them eternal life, and they shall never perish; no-one
> can snatch them out of my hand.
>
> (John 10:27–28)

So, I clasp this hand, struggle against despair, seek to delight in him and hang in there. It's a mystery of grace that the weaker my hands become, the more I am thrown towards the unbreakable clasp of God's hand. It's a greater mystery that I begin to be thankful for my growing weakness because I begin to learn that God's grace is, after all, sufficient, and that his power is demonstrated in my weakness. Like Paul, through the work of the Holy Spirit, the most amazing thing begins to happen: ' . . . for Christ's sake, I delight in weaknesses, in insults, in hardships, in persecutions, in difficulties. For when I am weak, then I am strong.'[5]

Francis Thomson's best-known poem is 'The Hound of Heaven'. Thomson was born in England in 1859 and much of his life was a confused wandering. He failed as a medical student and as a trainee priest, he left a trade as maker of surgical instruments, and could not hold down a job as a shoemaker's assistant. He was often homeless, suffering from tuberculosis and opium addiction. Although in his later life he was cared for in the homes of friends, he always experienced a kind of bewilderment with life and people. This poem expressed his experience of being 'chased' until he finally came to rest in God. The following lines capture a sense of learning to reject despair, and delighting in God's promises:

Whom wilt thou find to love ignoble thee,
Save Me, save only Me?
All which I took from thee
I did but take,
Not for thy harms,
But just that thou might'st seek it
In My arms.
All which thy child's mistake

Fancies as lost,
I have stored for thee at home:
Rise, clasp My hand, and Come.[6]

(Francis Thomson, 1859–1907)

Prayer

Lord Jesus, you understand our struggle with despair.
You know about hurt, fear and dread.
Good Shepherd, we rest in your hand, safe in your
    unbreakable grasp.
Warm us, with your grace, to delight in you and your
    sovereign care.
Clasp our weak hands and strengthen us each day to
    keep on trusting you.

Remember ...

On days when we struggle with despair, we know that Jesus knows how we feel and he holds us in his hand. We delight in him.

Feed on God's Word because it nourishes trust and
helps banish despair.

Attune your desires to God's ways and his purposes.

Delight in God's providence. God is governing and preserving our lives
in wisdom, power, and mercy.

Reject despair and hopelessness.

Reflect

seven

Awake or asleep?

We stay awake to God by remembering the past
and all that God has done through Jesus,
but also by remembering forwards,
having our eyes on what is to come.

As I write, it is the beginning of summer here in Australia. Spring is over, and its tempestuous storms and changes are settling into a long, hot, dry, and dangerous season. We fear summer at the same time as we enjoy it. We enjoy the beaches, the outdoor BBQs, the family get-togethers, the open-air concerts, and the long summer break when schools and workplaces shut down. We watch fireworks, laze by the water, and eat. But there is much to fear as well. We fear bushfires, the falling levels of water in our dams, and the visit of the English cricket team.

Humans adapt to the threats of summer in various ways, but our natural environment in Australia specializes in dealing with these extreme conditions. The great towering Australian gumtree thrives in the harsh summer. It reacts to bushfire by opening seed pods and scattering seeds which will sprout in the rich ashes. It can live through drought and heat, with root systems that are up to four times as wide as the tree, and can reach up to 40 metres underground. So the towering ragged tree we see standing firm is nourished by deep broad roots keeping it alive.

This is a good image for us when we face times in our lives that require us to stand firm. In times of illness or suffering we may feel as if we are standing still, going nowhere, doing nothing while others around us are busy, productive, and full of energy. The gumtree is a helpful image illustrating Paul's command:

> . . . put on the full armour of God, so that when the day of evil comes, you may be able to stand your ground, and after you have done everything, to stand.
>
> (Ephesians 6:13)

This verse makes me think of a strong sturdy gumtree, which may have branches missing, scars where it has been lashed by storms, twists and turns in its trunk, yet still stands firm with its roots deep underground and wide around it. If you have experienced the scars and lashings of suffering and illness, this image may resonate with you. It's no small thing to stand your ground, especially under pressure. Paul described his own experience of being under this kind of pressure:

> We were under great pressure, far beyond our ability to
> endure, so that we despaired even of life. Indeed, in our hearts
> we felt the sentence of death. But this happened that we
> might not rely on ourselves but on God, who raises the dead.
>
> (2 Corinthians 1:8–9)

Have you felt this awful sense of death creeping up on you?
I have. Have you had days when you despaired of your life? In
those times when our days seem far beyond our ability to endure,
we are not alone in our experience. Lately, when I have become
more housebound, I often think of those Christian brothers and
sisters around the world who are in prison for their faith, or who
suffer poverty and danger. At times like that I turn to prayer for
them, and it helps me realize I am not alone at all. I am part of a
huge community, a family, and in our kinship and suffering we
all seek to stand firm.

Paul says that this experience of suffering that pushes us to feel
the sentence of death in our hearts thrusts us upon God. It forces

us to rely on God because we have no resources left in ourselves. This is a good place to find ourselves because God is the one who raises the dead. He is the one who can bring life, hope, strength, and endurance into a place where we can see no future at all. He is able, even when we are not.

The appearance of the gumtree may be deceiving. Often in the height of summer, gumtrees look bedraggled and on the verge of death but they're not at all. Their roots sinking deep and broad ensure they are vibrantly alive. They will outlast the harsh weather and can wait for the rains to come. They are, metaphorically speaking, wide awake.

The Old Testament account of Joseph is the story of a man who stayed alert and awake to God under the pressure of suffering and the pressure of success. Although he was bullied and tossed into a pit by his brothers, sold to slave traders, and thrown into prison unjustly, Joseph maintained a trust in God. When he was thrust into power as a governor in Egypt he acted with wisdom.

When he was suddenly confronted by his brothers he acted with forgiveness.

Somehow, in the experience of seemingly meaningless suffering, he had stayed awake to God's purposes. As it turned out, he was able to ensure the survival of Israel. All his suffering culminated in something good as it fulfilled God's purposes. His brothers didn't have the same awareness; they were filled with guilt and fear. He said to them:

> 'Don't be afraid. Am I in the place of God? You intended to harm me, but God intended it for good to accomplish what is now being done, the saving of many lives. So then, don't be afraid. I will provide for you and your children.' And he reassured them and spoke kindly to them.
>
> (Genesis 50:19–21)

Joseph interpreted the meaning of his years of 'pointless' suffering in terms of the long-term purposes of God. No doubt, day after day in prison he could not imagine how it would end. It probably looked and felt dismal and meaningless. Nevertheless, he held on and trusted in God. He stayed awake.

How do we stay awake to God when we are confronted with life's struggles? One way is to be alert to the end of the story.

> By being aware of the future we can live through the present. The Bible's attitude to evil and suffering, unlike ours, is not dominated by the current evil and suffering that are around us in the world. Rather it is dominated by what is going to happen at the end of the world.[1]
>
> (Peter Hicks)

We stay awake to God by remembering the past and all that God has done through Jesus, but also by remembering forwards, having our eyes on what is to come.

The book of Revelation has been a source of deep comfort and strength since it was written for the persecuted Christians of the first century. It is brutally realistic, acknowledging that the world is full of evil and suffering. But what a glorious antidote for despair we find there as well. Jesus is Lord of all.[2] The day is coming when evil and suffering will end and things will be put right. At that time everyone will bow down before God, acknowledging the justice and glory of all that he has done.[3] In the new creation there will be no more suffering, and God's people will find a new home like no home they have ever dared to imagine.

> And I heard a loud voice from the throne saying, 'Now the dwelling of God is with men, and he will live with them. They will be his people, and God himself will be with them and be their God. He will wipe every tear from their eyes. There will be no more death or mourning or crying or pain, for the old order of things has passed away.'
>
> He who was seated on the throne said, 'I am making everything new!'

(Revelation 21:3–5)

What a vision! This is the kind of tough hope that keeps us awake to God and his purposes. This kind of awakening stirs in us a deep longing, an almost painful longing. This is what C. S. Lewis described as 'the inconsolable longing'.

> If I find in myself a desire which no experience in this world can satisfy, the most probable explanation is that I was made for another world.[4]
>
> (C. S. Lewis)

Being awake means experiencing this longing – for comfort and hope, for healing and wholeness, for home.

In his book from the Narnia series, *The Horse and His Boy*, C. S. Lewis tells the tale of the journey of Shasta and his horse Bree as they try to reach the land of Narnia. Throughout the story, Shasta and Bree feel out of place and have a sense they belong somewhere else – somewhere that is truly home. 'Narnia and the north!' becomes their rallying cry. As the journey develops, this deep motivation to find their true home keeps them moving northwards, no matter what dangers and misfortunes they experience. When I read this book I feel their longing, and I too realize that I am meant for another homeland, a place where I truly belong.

As Shasta nears his final destination and is trudging through a fog, unable to see his way clearly, he complains bitterly about all the troubles he has endured on the way – especially all the lions that kept turning up. His companion, unseen by him in the fog, is Aslan himself, who is symbolic of God. He explains to Shasta:

'I was the lion who forced you to join with Aravis, I was the cat who comforted you among the tombs. I was the lion who drove the jackals from you while you slept. I was the lion who gave the horses new strength of fear for the last mile so that you should reach King Lune in time. And I was the lion you do not remember who pushed the boat in which you lay, a child near death, so that it came to shore where a man sat, wakeful at night, to receive you.'[5]

Won't it be a wonderful moment when we too hear our story retold from the perspective of our Heavenly Father and his tender care for us through our entire journey, both in times of trouble and in times of ease?

But we become sleepy. I know that some days are slow and long and filled with inactivity. It can be easy to seek mindless distractions to pass the time. To some extent this is a necessary strategy, but there are days when I am aware that this leads to a kind of deadness in mind and spirit, and even a slow drift towards despair. There are days when I am tempted to thoughtlessly and desperately fill up my time rather than mindfully choose how I will use my time. I can slide into self-pity and resentment, or anger and jealousy at the health of others. I can begin to see things as the world might see them. I need waking up; I need to ask the Spirit to keep me awake and alert to God's love for me and God's purposes for me. I need self-control to pray, read God's Word, seek fellowship from other Christians, and to stay alert to God's Spirit as he counsels and convicts me.

> You and I have need of the strongest spell that can be found
> to wake us from the evil enchantment of worldliness.[6]
>
> (C. S. Lewis)

I have a friend who suffers from depression. Recently he shared with us that he needs to be disciplined to be mindful. He explained that this strategy helps him stay alive to now rather than being distracted by fears and worries about the future, or weighed down by sorrows and hurts from the past. This notion has been a help to me. It's very easy with a chronic and terminal illness to keep going over what you will miss out on in the future. I won't see my grandchildren, I might miss my daughter's wedding, I won't be able to travel with my husband anymore, and so on. Meanwhile, just outside my window it is a beautiful summer morning. The maple leaves have burst from their winter sleep, and my backyard is sprinkled with purple jacaranda blossoms. I hear a whip bird and his mate calling to each other. Today I will be driven down to see the river and to sit in the sun. There is a mango to mash for lunch. Some friends have emailed me to say hi. These simple things can help me stay awake to God's goodness. It's a choice between being awake to God or drowsily napping and slipping into despair.

Jesus is coming. Am I awake to that? Am I filled with anticipation? In one of Jesus' parables about the kingdom, he reminds his followers to stay awake and watch for his coming.

> 'No-one knows about that day or hour, not even the angels in
> heaven, nor the Son, but only the Father. Be on guard! Be
> alert! You do not know when that time will come. It's like a
> man going away: He leaves his house and puts his servants in

charge, each with his assigned task, and tells the one at the door to keep watch.

Therefore keep watch because you do not know when the owner of the house will come back – whether in the evening, or at midnight, or when the cock crows, or at dawn. If he comes suddenly, do not let him find you sleeping. What I say to you, I say to everyone: "Watch!"'

(Mark 13:32–37)

By God's grace, in the power of his Spirit within us, let's stay awake. Awake to the mercies of the present, awake to our Heavenly Father's care, awake to the Lordship of Jesus. Let's follow Jesus' command and be alert, keeping watch for him.

I am waiting for the dawning

I am waiting for the dawning
Of the bright and blessed day,
When the darksome night of sorrow
Shall have vanished far away –

When, forever with the Saviour,
Far beyond this vale of tears,
I shall swell the song of worship
Through the everlasting years . . .

I am waiting for the coming
Of the Lord who died for me;
O, his words have thrilled my spirit,
'I will come again for thee.'
I can almost hear his footfall
On the threshold of the door,
And my heart, my heart is longing.
To be with him evermore.[7]

(Samuel T. Francis, 1834–1925)

Prayer

Our Heavenly Father,
Help us to stay awake.
We grow drowsy and distracted as we wait for you,
At times our hearts are loaded down with sadness
    and struggle.
By your Spirit, strengthen us,
By your Word, nourish us,
Keep us longing for our true home,
Forever with you.

Remember …

We have God's Spirit, who helps keep us awake to who God is and how much he loves us. Being awake fills us with longing for what is to come when Jesus returns.

Remember the past – all that God has accomplished for us through Christ.

Remember the future – all that God has promised to accomplish through Christ.

Reject daily choices that tend to deaden heart and mind, and that encourage mindless passivity.

Stay awake and alert to the work of God's Spirit within you.

Reflect

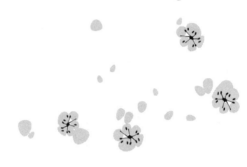

eight

Life and death

In laying down ourselves before him,
we take away with us
his life, his perspective,
and a longing that he be glorified.

Yesterday my little dog, Millie, who is playful, happy, and good to be around each day, killed a young bird. It was a young satin bowerbird. These beautiful and shy birds have brilliant blue-black eyes. They build a bower on the ground for their nest and decorate it with stolen bits and pieces, all bright blue. In the hot and gusty winds, this bird fell out of the sky and was not quite able to get itself up and away before my gentle little poodle flew at it and grabbed it by the throat. The mother bird chased and squawked, as did I, but the dog was completely overtaken by the instinct to catch and kill, and it did just that.

I feed the native birds each day and there are flocks of lorikeets, parrots, and doves that come down to my garden. There are whip birds, bowerbirds, and wrens that also hover around. It's peaceful and lovely. This was all shattered as my dog killed this young bird. What really surprised me was how upsetting it was to me, and still is. I hold a grudge against my dog for acting like a dog. Death is shocking when it happens right there in your face. I see death everyday on TV in the news and in 'who dunnits', and

I hardly raise an eyebrow, to my shame. But there, right in front of me, I found the death of one little bird terrible to see. And here, right in front of me, slow and sinister, is my approaching death. And I don't mind admitting it's a terrible thing to see coming.

Death is no surprise; we are all dying. Everyone I know and love will die. However, we usually live as if there is no death. We are confident in good fortune as we travel; we feel assured that in hospital we will get better; we plan our future with no thought of coming disaster. Until we are wrenched into reality by accident, disease, or misfortune. When that happens, it's unnerving.

It's also unnerving to be around people who are dying. I have one dear friend who simply cries every time we see each other. If I cough or struggle to swallow, she panics and becomes distressed. How strange to become a person who causes others distress just by being there. Mind you, I would be just like her if our roles were reversed.

Some of us are face to face with death with nowhere to run. Imminent or slow, we know death is coming. This tends to wrench us from the life everyone else is busily living around us. This can be an unrelenting experience. I don't know what it is like for other people but I still get a surprise every morning when I wake up and remember that I have MND; I can't say good morning to my husband; I can hardly manage a cup of tea; I can't do anything active and there's another long day ahead of me. Every morning is a fresh shock, and a little fresh stab of grief. Little ripples of death lap at me each morning.

Early on in this process I had to talk to myself sternly each morning. I remind myself that there are two ways of looking at this day. Either I am dying of MND, or I am living with MND. There is a simple but profound difference between those two perspectives. One is death, one is life. The choice is: Which perspective will I accept for myself today? One perspective opens the door to self-pity and withdrawal; the other allows for the possibility of enjoyment, creativity, laughter and relationship. I try to choose life freshly each morning. I don't always manage it.

Trying to think about your own death is a slippery business. On one level, you know you will die, like everyone else, and like everyone has before you, and it's a very cut-and-dried notion. On another level, and on a different day, there can be a moment of sheer terror and dread at the thought of your life ending, and this terror runs through you like a knife, and leaves you gasping in disbelief. No, no, it can't be! A different day sees you calm and patient, trusting God with the days and times of your life, facing the end with bold strength. Then one little thing happens – your daughter begins to plan her wedding, your grandson says 'when I grow up . . .', or your husband looks at you sadly – and all your courage goes to water at what you will be leaving undone, unsaid, unseen, and unfelt.

So my approach to this chapter about life and death changes each day. I had a day last week when I felt strong emotions rising to the surface to shatter my usual calmness; I was quietly and deeply raging against this disease, this decline, and the death that is coming. I didn't know it at first, I just felt deeply uneasy, but by the end of the day I recognized and named the deep rage I felt. And, for the first time, the following poem really did make sense to me. Dylan Thomas wrote it as his father was dying. As a Christian I never warmed to it, until now. Now I recognize the sheer rage against dying; the primal instinct to survive and live.

Do not go gentle into that good night
Do not go gentle into that good night,
Old age should burn and rave at close of day;
Rage, rage against the dying of the light.

Though wise men at their end know dark is right,
Because their words had forked no lightning they
Do not go gentle into that good night.

Good men, the last wave by, crying how bright
Their frail deeds might have danced in a green bay,
Rage, rage against the dying of the light.

Wild men who caught and sang the sun in,
And learn, too late, they grieved it on its way,
Do not go gentle into that good night.

Grave men, near death, who see with blinding sight
Blind eyes could blaze like meteors and be gay,
Rage, rage against the dying of the light.

And you, my father, there on that sad height,
Curse, bless, me now with your fierce tears, I pray.
Do not go gentle into that good night.
Rage, rage against the dying of the light.[1]

(Dylan Thomas, 1914–1953)

As Christians, perhaps we flinch from such strong reactions to dying. We seek the calm and patient trust, we exhort gentleness and joy. We want to be able to watch one another die without being too upset so we hope for a radiant glow, or a happy peacefulness. Yet I think there is a place in the pathway of death for some rage. Didn't the heavens shudder with anguish at the entry of sin into God's good creation? Didn't Jesus feel dread at the terrible task of his awful death to redeem this broken world? Well, then, a few episodes of raging seems acceptable.

We join with all creation when we groan at the struggle and difficulties of life. This morning on the news I saw images of refugees in Afghanistan with little shelter, barely any food or water, and no medical help. A woman was lying under a blanket, quietly groaning, in pain, dying. Her family had no way to help her. She just lay there groaning. What a symbol of the whole planet! Wracked with war, poverty, disease; destroying our resources; slowly suffocating in our own waste. Yes, the world is groaning, and we as individuals are groaning.

We know that the whole creation has been groaning as in the
pains of childbirth right up to the present time. Not only so,
but we ourselves, who have the firstfruits of the Spirit, groan
inwardly as we wait eagerly for our adoption as sons [and
daughters], the redemption of our bodies. For in this hope
we were saved.

(Romans 8:22–24)

Here's the difference for us. Yes, we groan along with all creation,
but our groaning has a 'waiting-ness' to it. It's not despair, but
longing. Childbirth is pain, but pain with hope. Our groaning is
like childbirth. We have hope; we have hope for life after death.
Yet we still seek meaning in the midst of our grief now. How to
live well when we know we are dying? How can we embrace life
with death at our heels?

Christians say some strange things, and one of the strangest is
that we seek death. We see our lives as a process of dying in
order to live. Jesus said we are to take up our cross and follow

him. He declared that whoever wants to save his life will lose it and whoever loses his life will find it. What does this kind of talk mean? Jesus was responding to Peter's declaration that Jesus is the Christ, the Messiah. Without pausing to congratulate Peter, he tells his disciples as clearly as possible that being the Messiah will involve death. Then he tells them that their own lives will include this path of death if they really want to be his followers.

> And he said, 'The Son of Man must suffer many things and be rejected by the elders, chief priests and teachers of the law, and he must be killed and on the third day be raised to life.'
> Then he said to them all: 'If anyone would come after me, he must deny himself and take up his cross daily and follow me. For whoever wants to save his life will lose it, but whoever loses his life for me will save it. What good is it for a man to gain the whole world, and yet lose or forfeit his very self?'
>
> (Luke 9:22–25)

This means we are all in the same boat: me with MND, or you perhaps with mental illness, or disappointment in your marriage, or trouble with your children, or with inner conflicts and fears. Whatever troubles you are facing, all of us are on a journey that tastes of death. As followers of Jesus we are not surprised, and we see these experiences as opportunities to lay down our lives at Jesus' feet. We give ourselves up to him; we accept the troubles as a part of life. In laying down ourselves before him we take away with us his life, his perspectives, and a longing that he be glorified. Suddenly, it's not about me, and whatever my struggles happen to be, it's about the Lord Jesus – following, serving, trusting, glorifying him. The apostle Paul says it this way:

I eagerly expect and hope that I will in no way be ashamed, but will have sufficient courage so that now as always Christ will be exalted in my body, whether by life or by death. For to me, to live is Christ and to die is gain.

(Philippians 1:20–21)

I have had time in this past year to listen more. I have listened to music and been to concerts. One experience that took me by surprise was going to the daytime concerts at the Sydney Opera House. Having been a full-time worker for so many years, I must say I had no idea that this subculture existed. There are people who use their days for what I was used to cramming into evenings and weekends. I went along to the daytime concerts and found myself as if I was in a crowd who had come to find Jesus. There I was amongst the frail, elderly, disabled, alone, sick, and needy. Along with all the other needy people, I sought music to lift my spirits, and often it did.

One of my favourite concerts was a performance of Prokofiev's version of *The Ugly Duckling*. Sung in Russian it seemed so much more haunting and powerful. I had the English version to follow, but even without it I think I could have guessed which part of the story was happening. Packed into this tale, and given extra beauty and pathos through Prokofiev's music, is the story of the swan brought up amongst ducklings. To them he is gangly, ugly, a misfit, and an outsider. He is excluded and persecuted and feels despairing at life. 'He spent the days trembling in the reeds, ravaged by anguish' said my English translation.

Poignantly, this also applied to many of us in the audience. What a beautiful moment in the music and the story when he sees himself as the other swans see him, as he grows up into himself and his true beauty, soaring away with them, amongst his own kind. 'It is possible to be born in the nest of a duck as long as the egg is that of a swan!' It's how I felt: imprisoned in this diseased body yet with the spirit of a swan, awaiting my true identity to be revealed, awaiting my real community. For now there is the waiting, the dying, and a growing sense of 'no longer being able to hold to the ground we stand on every day'.

The Swan

This drudgery of trudging through tasks
yet undone, heavily, as if bound,
is like the swan's not fully created walking.
And dying, this no longer being able
to hold to the ground we stand on every day,
like the swan's anxious letting himself down
Into the waters, which gently accept him
and, as if happy and already in the past,
draw away under him, ripple upon ripple,
while he, now utterly quiet and sure
and ever more mature and regal
and composed, is pleased to glide.[2]

(Rainer Maria Rilke, 1875–1926)

There's something here that resonates with my longing to die with dignity, staying composed and mature, ready to glide along the path that God has chosen to give me. Yet, somehow, it is apt to both quietly glide and deeply rage. While I struggle to hold to the ground I walk on, and wait for what is to come.

The Elizabethan poet, John Donne, expressed the longing to put death in its place:

Death be not proud, though some have called thee
Mighty and dreadful, for thou art not so . . .
One short sleep past, we wake eternally
And death shall be no more;
Death thou shalt die.[3]

(John Donne, 1572–1631)

1 Corinthians 15 is a glorious chapter about death being put in its place. Paul, harking back to Hosea, says, 'Where, O death, is your victory? Where, O death, is your sting?'[4] The rock solid ground of our hope is the resurrection of Jesus. In the words of Isaiah, given fresh application by Paul, 'Death has been swallowed up in victory.'[5] Because Jesus has been raised to life, I can have

hope that I will also receive a resurrection body, glorious and eternal, and I will speak and sing with the rest of God's people.

Listen, I tell you a mystery: We will not all sleep, but we will all be changed – in a flash, in the twinkling of an eye, at the last trumpet. For the trumpet will sound, the dead will be raised imperishable, and we will be changed. For the perishable must clothe itself with the imperishable, and the mortal with immortality. When the perishable has been clothed with the imperishable, and the mortal with immortality, then the saying that is written will come true: 'Death has been swallowed up in victory.'

'Where, O death, is your victory?
  Where, O death, is your sting?'

The sting of death is sin, and the power of sin is the law. But thanks be to God! He gives us the victory through our Lord Jesus Christ.

(1 Corinthians 15:51–57)

The following poem-prayer by John Donne contains a sense of hovering at the door, waiting for death, but he gives this a fresh and powerful perspective. While he waits, he is 'tuning himself'.

Hymn to God, My God, in My Sickness
Since I am coming to that holy room
Where with Thy choir of saints for evermore,
I shall be made Thy music; as I come
I tune the instrument here at the door,
And what I must do then, think here before.[6]

(John Donne, 1572–1631)

It is a beautiful way of viewing my future life with God, to be 'made Thy music', and the captivating image of my life here and now as a tuning of myself, as I stand at the door to that life. What is this process of tuning myself, of getting ready to be God's music? It's about the life I can live here and now; it's about the core of my identity, being 'in Christ'.[7] Being in Christ is the way, the only way, I become part of God's music.

John's Gospel is full of claims about life. Some are puzzling, some even seem outrageous. According to the opening verses, Jesus himself *is* Life: 'In him was life, and that life was the light of men.'[8] Jesus says of himself, 'I have come that they may have life, and have it to the full.'[9] He also makes the astounding claim, 'I am the resurrection and the life. He who believes in me will live, even though he dies; and whoever lives and believes in me will never die.'[10]

These are big claims! They arouse in me both longing and bewilderment. I want such life! Yet, I seem so bound and belittled by my real daily experience of living. These days, my daily routine is usually mundane and uneventful. I can easily slide into forgetting God's greatness and his grand purposes. Every now and then, God gives me such a shake that I open my eyes, take a deep breath, and see and feel things as they really are. It's usually suffering that blesses me with such a jolt.

But the man [sic] to whom God is All in all, who feels his life-roots hid with Christ in God, who knows himself the inheritor of all wealth, worlds, ages, and power – that man has begun to be alive indeed.

Let us in all the troubles of life remember that our one lack is life, that what we need is more life – more of the life-giving presence in us making us more, and more largely, alive.

When most oppressed, when most weary of life, as our unbelief would phrase it, let us remind ourselves that it is in truth the inroad and presence of death we are weary of. When most inclined to sleep, let us rouse ourselves to live. Of all things let us avoid the false refuge of a weary collapse, a hopeless yielding to things as they are. It is the life in us that is discontented. We need more of what is discontented, not more of the cause of the discontent.[11]

(George MacDonald)

Followers of Jesus have 'abundant life'. It's puzzling because, to be honest, when I look at most of us, we don't look like we have any secret that makes us more full of life than the next person.

This is deeply troubling to me. When I go to church I want to be bowled over by the sense that we share life here, we that have meaning, hope, joy, and honesty that the rest of the world doesn't possess. To my disappointment, sometimes when we Christians meet together we seem shallow, mediocre, light-weight, thoughtless, and either glum or silly. When we do seek to make sense of the huge problems life holds, we tend to be simplistic, brief, and prayer-less. I can walk away discouraged when I want to be refreshed and nourished. I am critical of myself for the very same reasons, and I know that I often choose to live a lightweight distraction-filled life when I could be sinking more deeply into God's Word and his grace-filled relationship with me.

In MacDonald's words again:

> We are vessels of life, but we are not yet full of the wine of life.[12]

(George MacDonald)

I am meant for life, and as a follower of Jesus, I have the taste for it. These days when I can't eat much anymore because my tongue is a dead muscle and my throat is a weak muscle, I can't be bothered with 'no frills' chocolate, I want the handmade rich chocolate that I can slowly savour and allow to trickle down my throat. I've tasted it now, and the other stuff is not worth the effort. I've tasted real life now in my relationship with God, and the other kind of life is so 'no frills' it's not worth the trouble of pursuing it.

What do I have now, even if only a taste? I have relationship with a loving Father who knows me deeply, loves me relentlessly, and delights in blessing me. I have in Jesus a brother and a high priest who knows how it feels to walk this earthly messy road; I have in Jesus, the Son of Man, a teacher full of compassion and patience; I have in Jesus a Lord and King blazing with authority and power; I have in Jesus a resurrected Saviour, the Son of God, who will return to make all things new in complete victory over all the forces of evil and injustice, suffering, and sorrow. I may only have a taste, but what a taste it is! So much to savour and allow to trickle through my mind and spirit.

Meanwhile, I will seek to be 'joyful in hope, patient in affliction, faithful in prayer'.[13] This is how I tune myself, for the music I will become.

None Other Lamb

None other Lamb, none other Name,
None other hope in earth or heaven or sea,
None other hiding-place from guilt and shame,
None beside Thee!

My faith burns low, my hope burns low;
Only my heart's desire cries out in me
By the deep thunder of its want and woe,
Cries out to Thee.

Lord, Thou art Life, though I be dead;
Love's fire Thou art, however cold I be;
Nor heaven have I, nor place to lay my head,
Nor home, but Thee.[14]   (Christina Rossetti, 1830–1894)

Prayer

Fill me with your life, Lord Jesus,
Make me alive to who you are: my Lord, my Brother,
    my Saviour and my King.
Make me alive to who I am: loved, held, protected,
    and empowered by you.
Then let me, full of true life, see and know things
    as they really are.

Remember …

The rock solid ground on which our life rests is the resurrection of Jesus. Because he lives, we also live, and our eternal life is assured.

Understand your suffering as part of the grief experienced by all of creation as it lies under the heaviness of sin and brokenness.

Seek to follow the apostle Paul's example: 'to live is Christ and to die is gain.'[15]

See your groaning as a part of waiting; waiting for the new creation where all will be made right under Christ.

Hold fast to the hope that Christ has the victory over death, and he has promised us a new and glorious body.

Reflect

'**Remember these things**, O Jacob,
>   for you are my servant, O Israel.
I have made you, you are my servant;
>   O Israel, **I will not forget you**.
I have swept away your offences like a cloud,
>   your sins like the morning mist.
Return to me,
>   for I have redeemed you.'

Sing for joy, O heavens, for the LORD has done this;
>   shout aloud, O earth beneath.
Burst into song, you mountains,
>   you forests and all your trees,
for the LORD has redeemed Jacob,
>   he displays his glory in Israel.

>   (Isaiah 44:21–23, my emphasis)

Notes

Introduction
1. Dr Martyn Lloyd-Jones, quoted in John Piper, *Future Grace* (Multnomah Press, 1995), p. 304.
2. Richard J. Mouw, *Calvinism in the Las Vegas Airport* (Zondervan, 2004), p. 57.
3. Ibid., p. 80.

Chapter 1. Beauty and ugliness
1. G. M. Hopkins, 'Pied Beauty', in G. M. Hopkins, Catherine Philips (ed.), *Gerard Manley Hopkins: Selected Poetry* (OUP, 2008), p. 117. Used by permission of Oxford University Press on behalf of The British Province of the Society of Jesus.
2. John 13:31.
3. Luke 4:21.
4. Romans 8:22–23.
5. Attributed to Richard Keen, from 'How firm a foundation', http://www.ccli.com/songsearch. Public domain.

Chapter 2. Silence and speech
1. Lord Alfred Tennyson, from 'Break, Break, Break', in Alfred Tennyson, Adam Roberts (ed.), *Tennyson: The Major Works* (OUP, 2009), p. 96. Used by permission of Oxford University Press.
2. John 20:10–16.
3. Rainer Maria Rilke, 'The quieting of Mary with the resurrected one', in *The Essential Rilke*, trans. Galway Kinnell and Hannah Liebmann (Ecco Press, 2000), p. 63. Used by permission of HarperCollins Publishers.
4. Hebrews 1:1–2.
5. Genesis 1.
6. Deuteronomy 11:18.
7. John 6:68.
8. Isaac Watts, 'Come, let us join our cheerful songs', http://www.ccli.com/songsearch. Public domain.

Chapter 3. Fear and trust

1. Rhonda Watson, 'Fear', © 2009, Rhonda Watson.
2. John 15:16.
3. John 15:14, 17.
4. Helen Keller, from the website, http://www.brainyquote.com/quotes/quotes/h/helenkelle162480.html
5. Exodus 19:16–19.
6. S. E. Porter, *New Dictionary of Biblical Theology* (IVP, 2000), p. 497.
7. Genesis 26:24, Matthew 10:31, Mark 5:36, John 14:27, to cite a few.
8. See Andrew Cameron and ed. Brian Rosner for this concept, *Still Deadly: Ancient Cures for the 7 Sins* (Aquila Press, 2007), p. 33.
9. St Augustine, from the website, http://www.beliefnet.com/Quotes/Christian/S/St-Augustine-Of-Hippo/Trust-The-Past-To-Gods-Mercy-The-Present-To-God.aspx
10. Sidney Lanier, from 'The Marshes of Glynn' in Sidney Lanier, *Hymns of the Marshes*, http://www.poemhunter.com/poem/hymns-of-the-marshes. Public domain.
11. Isaac Watts, 'O God our help in ages past', http://www.ccli.com/songsearch. Public domain.

Chapter 4. Thankfulness and bitterness

1. Oswald Chambers, *My Utmost for His Highest* (Discovery House Publishers, 1989), p. 215.
2. Quoted in Richard J. Mouw, *Calvinism in the Las Vegas Airport* (Zondervan, 2004), p. 77.
3. Ephesians 4:31–32: 'Get rid of all bitterness, rage and anger, brawling and slander, along with every form of malice. Be kind and compassionate to one another, forgiving each other, just as in Christ God forgave you.'
4. Luke 21:1–4.
5. Leviticus 7:13–15.
6. See especially Romans 5:1–5.
7. Graham Kendrick, 'Lord, you've been good to me', © 2001, Make Way Music. Used by permission.
8. Martin Rinkart, tr. Catherine Winkworth, 'Now thank we all our God', http://www.ccli.com/songsearch. Public domain.

Chapter 5. Joy and grief

1. James 1:2.

2. Carl Sandburg, 'Joy' from *Chicago Poems*, in Carl Sandburg, *The Complete Poems of Carl Sandburg* (Harcourt, 2003), p. 51. Copyright © 1916, Holt, Rinehart and Winston and renewed 1944 by Carl Sandbury. Used by permission of Houghton Mifflin Harcourt Publishing Company.
3. John 11:33–35.
4. Luke 13:34.
5. Luke 7:11–17.
6. Mark 10:21.
7. Denise Levertov, 'Talking to Grief' in Denise Levertov, *Poems 1972–1982* (New Directions, 2001), p. 120. Copyright © 1978, Denise Levertov. Used by permission of New Directions Publishing Corp.
8. Leviticus 23:40.
9. Deuteronomy 14:23.
10. Deuteronomy 14:26.
11. Habakkuk 3:16.
12. George MacDonald, M. Phillips (ed.), *Your Life in Christ* (Bethany House, 2005), p. 74.
13. John 3:16.
14. C. S. Lewis, quoted in C. Kilby, *A Mind Awake* (Bles, 1968), p. 26.
15. See Revelation 5:6–14.
16. Henry van Dyke, 'Hymn of Joy', http://www.ccli.com/songsearch. Public domain.

Chapter 6. Delight and despair

1. J. I. Packer, *Concise Theology* (Tyndale House Publishers, 1993), p. 55.
2. Luke 11:1ff.
3. Matthew 6:6–8.
4. Matthew 26:38.
5. 2 Corinthians 12:10.
6. Francis Thomson, from 'The Hound of Heaven', http://www.ccli.com/songsearch. Public domain.

Chapter 7. Awake or asleep?

1. Peter Hicks, *The Message of Evil and Suffering* (IVP, 2006), p. 23.
2. Revelation 1:12–18.
3. Revelation 15:2–4.
4. C. S. Lewis, quoted in C. Kilby, *A Mind Awake* (Bles, 1968), p. 22.

5. C. S. Lewis, *The Horse and His Boy* from 'The Chronicles of Narnia' (Collins, 2001), p. 281.
6. C. S. Lewis, *The Weight of Glory*, cited in C. Kilby, *A Mind Awake* (Bles, 1968) p. 26.
7. Samuel T. Francis, 'I am waiting for the dawning', http://www.ccli.com/songsearch. Public domain.

Chapter 8. Life and death

1. Dylan Thomas, 'Do not go gentle into that good night', in Ed Untermyer, *Albatross Book of Verse* (Collins 1960), p. 629. Copyright © 1952, Dylan Thomas in *The Poems of Dylan Thomas* (New Directions, 1971). Used by permission of New Directions Publishing Corp.
2. Rainer Maria Rilke, 'The Swan' in *The Essential Rilke*, tr. Galway Kinnell and Hannah Liebmann (Ecco Press, 2000), p. 15. Copyright © 2000, Galway Kinnell and Hannah Liebmann. Used by permission of HarperCollins Publishers.
3. John Donne, 'Divine Sonnet X', in A. W. Allison (ed.) et al., *Norton Anthology of Poetry* (Norton & Co., 1975), p. 98. Public domain.
4. 1 Corinthians 15:55.
5. 1 Corinthians 15:54.
6. John Donne, 'Hymn to God, My God, in My Sickness', in A. W. Allison (ed.) et al., *Norton Anthology of Poetry*, (Norton & Co., 1975), p. 98. Public domain.
7. Ephesians 2:4–7.
8. John 1:4.
9. John 10:10.
10. John 11:25–26.
11. George MacDonald, Michael Phillips (ed.), *Your Life in Christ* (Bethany House, 2005), p. 73.
12. Ibid., p. 72.
13. Romans 12:12.
14. Christina Rossetti, 'None Other Lamb', http://www.ccli.com/songsearch. Public domain.
15. Philippians 1:21.